YA
507.8
GAR

BLUE ISLAND PUBLIC LIBRARY
BLUE ISLAND, ILLINOIS

Earth Science!
BEST SCIENCE PROJECTS

Weather Science Fair Projects

Using Sunlight, Rainbows, Ice Cubes, and More

Robert Gardner

Enslow Publishers, Inc.
40 Industrial Road   PO Box 38
Box 398   Aldershot
Berkeley Heights, NJ 07922   Hants GU12 6BP
USA   UK

http://www.enslow.com

Copyright © 2005 by Robert Gardner

All rights reserved.

No part of this book may be reproduced by any means without the written permission of the publisher.

Library of Congress Cataloging-in-Publication Data

Gardner, Robert, 1929–
   Weather science fair projects using sunlight, rainbows, ice cubes, and more / Robert Gardner.
       p. cm. — (Earth science!)
   Includes bibliographical references and index.
   ISBN 0-7660-2361-3
   1. Weather—Experiments—Juvenile literature. 2. Science projects—Juvenile literature. I. Title. II. Earth science! (Berkeley Heights, N.J.)
   QC981.3G42 2005
   551.6'078—dc22
                                                                                           2004015722

Printed in the United States of America

10 9 8 7 6 5 4 3 2 1

To Our Readers: We have done our best to make sure all Internet Addresses in this book were active and appropriate when we went to press. However, the author and the publisher have no control over and assume no liability for the material available on those Internet sites or on other Web sites they may link to. Any comments or suggestions can be sent by e-mail to comments@enslow.com or to the address on the back cover.

Illustration Credits: All illustrations by Tom LaBaff, except pp. 30, 44, 49 by Stephen F. Delisle.

Photo Credit: National Oceanic and Atmospheric Administration, p. 113.

Cover photo: © 2004 Dynamic Graphics

Contents

Introduction 5

1 *Weather Maps and Instruments* 9
    1.1   Weather Maps 10
    1.2   Weather Instruments You Can Make 13
    1.3   What is the Rainfall Content of Snow? . . . 22
    1.4   Other Instruments for Your
          Weather Station 24

2 *Earth's Atmosphere and
the Sky We See* 32
    2.1   What Percentage of Air Is Oxygen? 34
    2.2   Blue Sky, Yellow Sun, and
          Red Sunsets. 40
    2.3   Rainbows in the Sky and Elsewhere 43
    2.4   Bending Light to Make a "Rainbow" . . . 45
    2.5   Refraction at Sunrise, Sunset,
          and in a Cup 50

3 *Humidity, Sunshine, and Weather* 52
    3.1   Finding the Dew Point 54
    3.2   Measuring Humidity with
          a Hygrometer. 59
    3.3   Weather Records at Your
          Weather Station 64
    3.4   Why Is Summer Hot and
          Winter Cold? 68
    3.5   The Effect of Angle on the
          Absorption of Radiant Energy 70

3.6	The Sun's Effect on Earth's Air	....	73
3.7	Hot Air, Cold Air, and Volume	....	74
3.8	Transferring Energy to Water and Soil	...	77
3.9	The Effect of Color on Radiant Energy Absorption	....	81
3.10	Models of the Hydrologic Cycle	....	85
3.11	Factors Affecting the Evaporation of Water	....	88

4 Air and Wind Patterns on a Spinning Globe 91
4.1	Stable and Unstable Air	92
4.2	What Causes Winds?	94
4.3	Winds: A Complication	96

5 Clouds and Stormy Weather 105
5.1	Recipe for a Cloud	106
5.2	Making a Cloud	108
5.3	Thunder and Lightning	118
5.4	A Liquid Tornado	120

6 Forecasting Weather 122

Questions and Answers 124

Science Supply Companies 125

Further Reading and Internet Addresses 126

Index 127

Introduction

How do clouds form? Why does wind blow? How do thunderstorms develop? What conditions make rain or snow? The experiments in this book will help you better understand the forces behind Earth's weather.

Most of the materials you will need to carry out the projects and experiments described in this book can be found in your home. Several of the experiments may require items that you can buy in a supermarket, a hobby or toy shop, a hardware store, or one of the science supply companies listed in the appendix. Some may call for articles that you may be able to borrow from your school's science department.

Occasionally, you will need someone to help you with an experiment that requires more than one pair of hands. It would be best if you work with friends or adults who enjoy experimenting as much as you do. In that way you will both enjoy what you are doing. **If any danger is involved in doing an experiment, it will be made known to you. In some cases, to avoid any danger to you, you will be asked to work with an adult. Please do so.** We do not want you to take any chances that could lead to an injury.

Like any good scientist, you will find it useful to record your ideas, notes, data, and anything you can conclude from your experiments in a notebook. By so doing, you can keep track of the information you gather and the conclusions you reach. It will allow you to refer to experiments you have done and help you in doing other projects in the future.

SCIENCE FAIRS

Some of the projects in this book are followed by a section called Science Project Ideas. These ideas may be appropriate for a science fair. However, judges at such fairs do not reward projects or experiments that are simply copied from a book. For example, a fluffy cotton model of a cloud would probably not impress judges unless it was done in a novel or creative way. A report of an experiment to explain how raindrops form in a cloud would receive much more consideration than pieces of cotton glued to a blue background.

Science fair judges tend to reward creative thought and imagination. However, it is difficult to be creative or imaginative unless you are really interested in your project, so choose something that appeals to you. Consider, too, your own ability and the cost of materials needed for the project.

If you decide to use a project found in this book for a science fair, you will need to find ways to modify or extend the project. This should not be difficult because you will probably find that as you do these projects, ideas for new experiments will come to mind. These new experiments could make excellent science fair projects, particularly because they spring from your own mind and are interesting to you.

Introduction

If you decide to enter a science fair and have never done so before, you should read some of the books listed in the further reading section. Some of these books deal specifically with science fairs and will provide plenty of helpful hints and lots of useful information that will enable you to avoid the pitfalls that sometimes plague first-time entrants. You will learn how to prepare appealing reports that include charts and graphs, how to set up and display your work, how to present your project, and how to talk to judges and visitors.

SAFETY FIRST

Most of the projects included in this book are perfectly safe. However, the following safety rules are well worth reading before you start any project.

1. Do any experiments or projects, whether from this book or of your own design, under the supervision of a science teacher or other knowledgeable adult.

2. Read all instructions carefully before proceeding with a project. If you have questions, check with your supervisor before going any further.

3. Maintain a serious attitude while conducting experiments. Fooling around can be dangerous to you and to others.

4. Wear approved safety goggles when doing anything that might injure your eyes.

5. Do not eat or drink while experimenting.

6. Have a first aid kit nearby while you are experimenting.

7. Do not put your fingers or any object other than properly designed electrical connectors into electrical outlets.

8. Never experiment with household electricity except under the supervision of a knowledgeable adult.

9. Do not touch a lit high-wattage bulb. Also, never let water droplets come in contact with a hot lightbulb. Lightbulbs produce light but they also produce heat and will shatter if suddenly cooled.

10. Never look directly at the sun. It can cause permanent damage to your eyes.

11. The liquid in some thermometers is mercury. It is dangerous to touch mercury or to breathe mercury vapor, and such thermometers have been banned in many states. When doing these experiments, use only non-mercury thermometers, such as those filled with alcohol. If you have a mercury thermometer in the house, **ask an adult** if it can be taken to a local mercury thermometer exchange location.

12. Practice patience as you experiment. Experiments performed with care lead to results in which you can have confidence.

Chapter **1**

Weather Maps and Instruments

Weather is forever changing. If not today, then soon. In a speech to the New England Society in 1876, Mark Twain had this to say about weather in New England: "There is a sumptuous variety about New England weather. . . . In the spring I have counted one hundred and thirty-six different kinds of weather inside of four-and-twenty hours."

Of course, Mark Twain was noted for exaggeration; however, changes in weather are frequent. Meteorologists, scientists who study weather, have the difficult task of trying to forecast the weather. They study the atmosphere—the mass of air surrounding Earth—and try to predict how it affects our weather. The National Weather Service hires meteorologists to provide weather information for the entire country. After listening to a public weather report, people may decide to cancel a picnic, evacuate their homes because of an approaching hurricane, or seek shelter in a storm cellar as a tornado draws near.

Experiment 1.1

Weather Maps

Materials

- ✓ daily newspaper that has a daily weather map
- ✓ scrapbook or photo album

Newspapers usually publish a daily weather map. In the United States the map shows most of North America. On the map you will usually find the predicted temperature (high and low for the day) near some major cities. You will also find symbols like those shown in Figure 1. The symbols indicate the location of centers of high and low atmospheric pressure, weather fronts, and precipitation (light rain, showers, snow, ice, thunderstorms). Sometimes the maps are color-coded to show the day's high temperature over different regions of the country.

Weather fronts are places where large air masses collide. For example, a cold air mass from northern Canada may collide with a warmer air mass to the south. The cold, denser air will push under the warmer, less dense air and lift it. If the cold

Weather Maps and Instruments

high pressure — H

low pressure — L

warm front

occluded front

cold front

stationary front

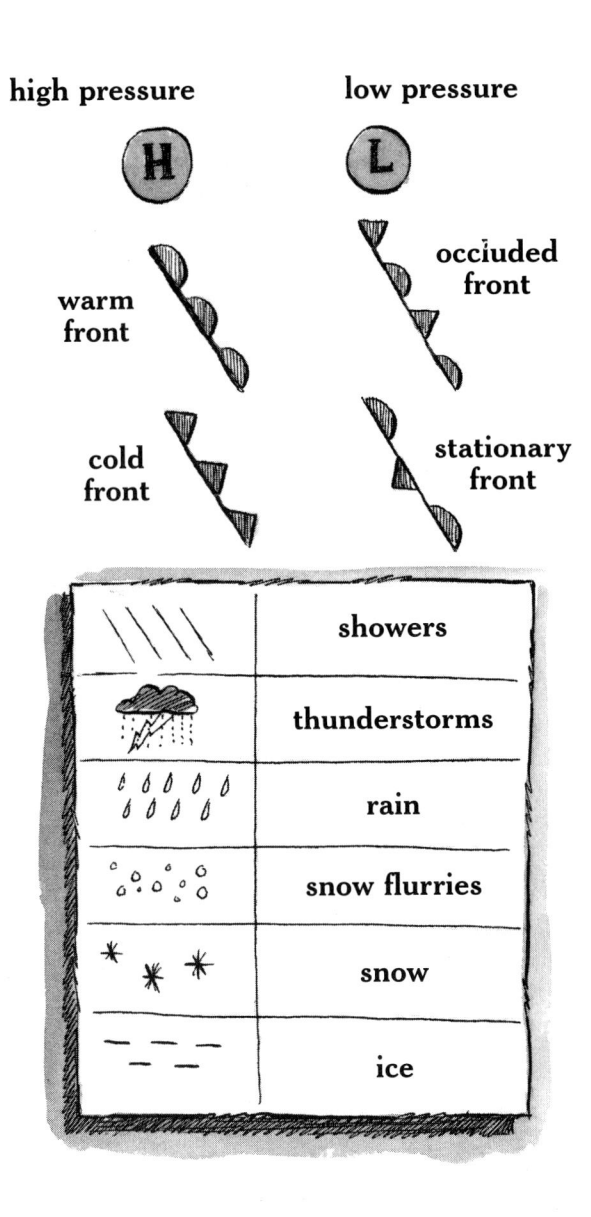

/////	showers
⛈	thunderstorms
,,,,,	rain
° ° ° °	snow flurries
✱ ✱ ✱	snow
— — —	ice

Figure 1.

These symbols are found on weather maps. Check your newspaper's key, as symbols may vary.

air advances, we have a cold front. If the air masses don't move, we have a stationary front. If the cold air retreats as warm air moves over it, we have a warm front. When a cold front, which generally moves faster than a warm front, overtakes a warm front and lifts the warmer air, we have an occluded front.

You will soon learn more about weather and its qualities—such as atmospheric pressure, wind, precipitation, clouds, and so on. But for now, ask a parent for permission to cut out the daily weather map from the family newspaper. Keep these maps in a scrapbook or photo album, in order, so that you can see how fronts, precipitation, and highs and lows move and change from day to day. Observe these maps each day for a month or more. Do weather patterns seem to move in any particular direction across the United States? If they do, in what direction do they move? Record all your findings in a notebook. Over a number of months, you can discover whether weather patterns move more rapidly in summer or winter.

Weather Maps and Instruments

Experiment 1.2

Weather Instruments You Can Make

Materials

- ✓ **an adult**
- ✓ safety glasses
- ✓ work gloves
- ✓ tape measure
- ✓ 15 cm x 45 cm (6 in × 18 in) plywood, 1/2 in thick
- ✓ long, thin screw and washer
- ✓ drill and bit
- ✓ coping saw or jigsaw
- ✓ 2 in × 4 in post, 1.2 m (4 ft) long
- ✓ watch or clock
- ✓ shovel
- ✓ 15 cm × 15 cm (6 in × 6 in) piece of 3/4-in plywood
- ✓ hammer
- ✓ 2 nails
- ✓ tin snips
- ✓ large tin can
- ✓ pliers
- ✓ car
- ✓ large jar or can with straight sides
- ✓ narrow olive jar
- ✓ masking tape
- ✓ water
- ✓ cup
- ✓ pencil
- ✓ ruler

To begin to analyze and, later, forecast local weather, you can make a weather station and keep a daily record of the weather. Some of the weather instruments you will need are easy to make. Others can be purchased or borrowed from a school science department. With these instruments, you will be able to measure wind direction and speed, rainfall, air temperature, air pressure, and humidity.

To find the direction from which the wind is blowing, you can make a wind vane. To measure wind speed, you can make an anemometer. To measure rainfall, you can make a rain gauge.

A WIND VANE TO MEASURE WIND DIRECTION

Ask an adult to help you cut a large arrow (Figure 2a) from a piece of 15 cm × 45 cm (6 in × 18 in) 1/2-inch-thick plywood. Move the arrow back and forth on your finger until you find its balance point. **Ask the adult** to drill a hole through the arrow at the balance point, using a drill bit that is slightly larger than the screw you will use to attach the wind vane to a post. A washer between the post and the wind vane will allow the vane to spin freely.

Mount your wind vane on a wooden post about 1.2 m (4 ft) tall. Since the wind's direction often changes when it blows around trees or buildings, the post should be out in the open. Bury the bottom end of the post in a hole about 45 cm (18 in) deep.

To assign directions to the wind, you need to know the location of true north (the direction to the North Pole). You can find it by using the post's shadow. To do this, mark the length of the post's shadow at five-minute intervals during the hour around midday (when the sun reaches its highest

Weather Maps and Instruments

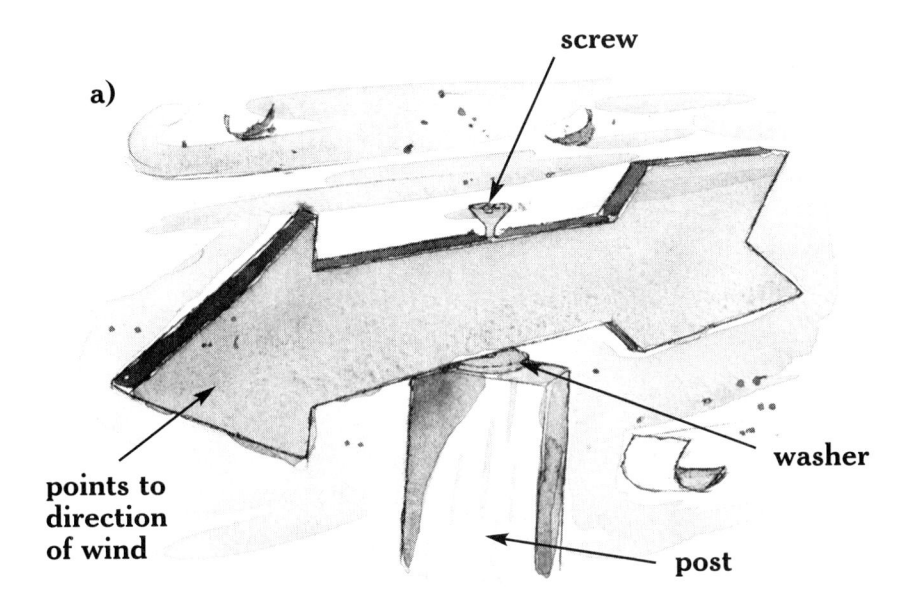

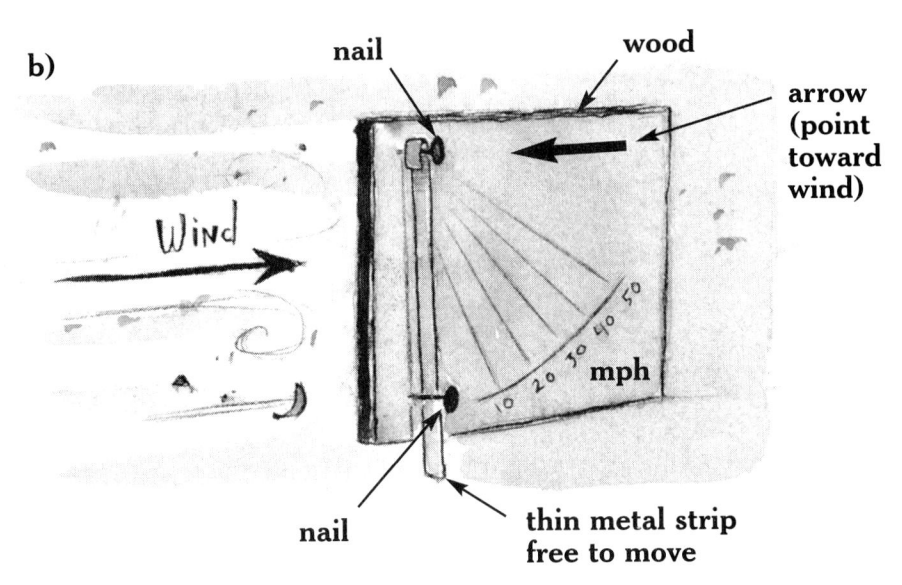

Figure 2.
You can make your own a) wind vane and b) anemometer.

point in the sky). **Never look directly at the sun! It can damage your eyes.**

A line from the post to the end of its shortest shadow will point toward true north. Devise a way to indicate that direction on the post. Once you have located true north, how can you find south, east, and west?

On some days, the wind may not be strong enough to move the wind vane. But when there is at least a moderate breeze, the vane should point to the direction from which the wind is blowing. Meteorologists always give the wind direction as the direction *from* which the air is moving. For example, a northeast wind blows from the northeast to the southwest.

How can you determine the direction of a light wind?

AN ANEMOMETER TO MEASURE WIND SPEED

An anemometer is used to measure wind speed. The anemometer used at weather stations has three cups that catch the wind and rotate. A small generator at the base of the shaft sends an electric current to a meter dial inside the station. The faster the cups rotate, the larger the electric current.

You can make a different kind of anemometer from a small piece of wood about 15 cm (6 in) square, as shown in Figure 2b. **Put on safety glasses** and hammer nails partway into two adjacent corners of the wood. **Wearing heavy gloves,** use tin snips to cut a strip of metal from a tin can. **Be careful; the metal can be sharp.** The strip should be about

Weather Maps and Instruments

2.5 cm (1 in) wide and 20 cm (8 in) long. Use pliers to bend one end of the strip loosely around a nail. When you hold the wood up, the other end of the strip should rest on the other nail. This is your zero point. Draw an arrow on the wood to show which way to aim the anemometer. When the anemometer is pointed into the wind, the strip will be blown up at an angle.

To calibrate your anemometer, you will need a car, a calm day (no wind), and **an adult driver.** Find a straight road where there is very little traffic. Ask your driver to go exactly 20 kilometers per hour (kph) or 12 miles per hour (mph). Hold the anemometer vertically out the window, with the arrow pointing in the direction you are going. Draw a pencil line on the wood to show how far the strip is moved by the air moving past the car. Make other lines when the car is traveling 40 kph (25 mph), 60 kph (37 mph), and 80 kph (50 mph).

Test your anemometer on the next windy day. How much does the wind speed change from one minute to the next?

The Beaufort scale uses the movement of smoke, leaves, and trees as an estimate of wind speed. Compare measurements on your anemometer with the Beaufort scale shown in Table 1.

Table 1. THE BEAUFORT SCALE

Beaufort Scale Number: **0**
Wind: **calm**
Observations: **Smoke rises vertically**
Wind Speed: **(mph)**   **(kph)**
                 0   0

Beaufort Scale Number: **1**
Wind: **light air**
Observations: **Wind direction given by smoke but not by wind vane**
Wind Speed: **(mph)**   **(kph)**
                1–3   1–5

Beaufort Scale Number: **2**
Wind: **light breeze**
Observations: **Leaves rustle; wind vane moves; can feel wind on your face**
Wind Speed: **(mph)**   **(kph)**
                4–7   6–11

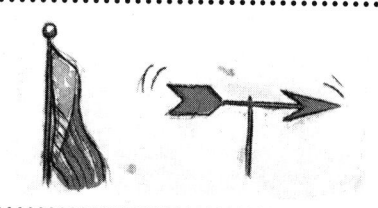

Beaufort Scale Number: **3**
Wind: **gentle breeze**
Observations: **Wind extends small flags; leaves are in constant motion**
Wind Speed: **(mph)**   **(kph)**
                8–12   12–19

Beaufort Scale Number: **4**
Wind: **moderate breeze**
Observations: **Small branches move; dust and loose paper lifted**
Wind Speed: **(mph)**   **(kph)**
                13–18   20–29

Beaufort Scale Number: **5**
Wind: **fresh breeze**
Observations: **Small trees with leaves sway, wavelets form on lakes**
Wind Speed: **(mph)**   **(kph)**
                19–24   30–39

Beaufort Scale Number: **6**
Wind: **strong breeze**
Observations: **Large branches move; utility lines seem to whistle**
Wind Speed: **(mph)**   **(kph)**
                25–31   40–50

Beaufort Scale Number: **7**
Wind: **near gale**
Observations: **Whole trees move; some difficulty walking into wind**
Wind Speed: **(mph)** **(kph)**
32–38 51–61

Beaufort Scale Number: **8**
Wind: **gale**
Observations: **Twigs break off trees; difficult to walk against wind**
Wind Speed: **(mph)** **(kph)**
39–46 62–74

Beaufort Scale Number: **9**
Wind: **strong gale**
Observations: **Slight damage to buildings**
Wind Speed: **(mph)** **(kph)**
47–54 75–87

Beaufort Scale Number: **10**
Wind: **storm**
Observations: **Trees uprooted, considerable damage to buildings**
Wind Speed: **(mph)** **(kph)**
55–63 88–102

Beaufort Scale Number: **11**
Wind: **violent storm**
Observations: **Widespread damage**
Wind Speed: **(mph)** **(kph)**
64–73 103–118

Beaufort Scale Number: **12**
Wind: **hurricane**
Observations: **Extreme destruction of property**
Wind Speed: **(mph)** **(kph)**
74+ 118+

A RAIN GAUGE TO MEASURE RAINFALL

A large jar or can with straight sides will allow you to collect rain in order to measure rainfall (see Figure 3a). A peanut butter jar or coffee can works well. A mayonnaise jar is not suitable because its mouth is smaller than the rest of the jar. Light rainfalls are difficult to measure with a wide-mouth collecting jar or can. To make a more accurate measurement, use a second jar (Figure 3b) that is as narrow as possible. An olive jar is ideal.

To mark a scale on the narrow jar, pour water into the wide-mouth jar or can until it is exactly 2.5 cm (1 in) deep. Pour that water into the narrow jar. Use a strip of masking tape to make a scale on the outside of the narrow jar. Mark the height of the water as 2.5. Then divide the space into five equal parts so that you can measure half centimeters (fifths of an inch) of rainfall.

Place the large container outside in an open spot away from trees, bushes, and buildings. You might want to attach the container to a small stake so that it will not be upset by the wind or a thirsty animal.

Check your rain gauge every morning, because it often rains at night. When you find rain in the container, untie it and measure the amount of water with the calibrated narrow jar. Most storms deposit less than one inch of rain. How can you measure the rainfall if there is more than one inch?

Weather Maps and Instruments

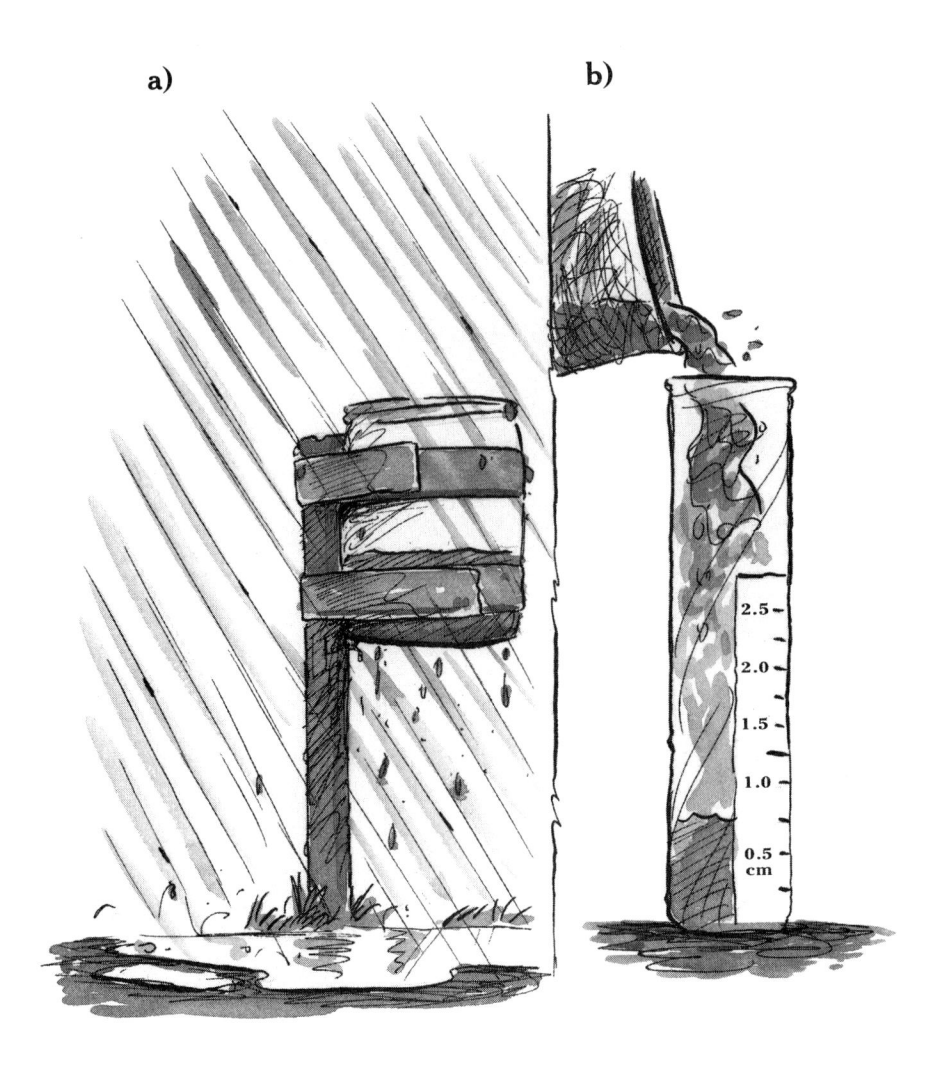

Figure 3.

A homemade rain gauge consists of two vessels, one with a large diameter (a), and one with a small diameter (b). A scale attached to the narrow jar will allow you to measure small amounts of rainfall.

In winter, when the temperature in clouds is very cold, snowflakes form and fall instead of rain. In the next experiment, you will learn how to convert inches of snow into inches of rain.

Science Project Ideas

- Devise another way to find true north.
- Using your wind vane, design an experiment to find the direction of the prevailing wind where you live. Does it change from season to season?

Experiment 1.3

What Is the Rainfall Content of Snow?

Materials

- ✓ ruler or yardstick
- ✓ shovel
- ✓ tall coffee can

In the winter, precipitation often falls as snow. However, you can convert centimeters (inches) of snow to centimeters (or inches) of rain. You will need to measure snow depths with a ruler or yardstick. After the storm has passed, find an open

Weather Maps and Instruments

area away from trees and buildings. Push the ruler straight down through the snow until it strikes the hard ground. After reading the depth, shovel away the snow until you have a small bare spot. Now you can measure the next snowfall in the same place without the snow layer from the first storm underneath.

It is important for meteorologists to know the water content of the snow that falls during the winter. When spring arrives, water from melting snow runs into rivers and lakes. If there is a lot of snow and it melts quickly, dangerous floods can result.

To find the rainfall content of snow, you will need a tall coffee can. Fill the can with the loose snow that fell; do not pack it down. Bring the can inside; allow the snow to melt. Measure the depth of water and the depth of the can. Then figure out how much snow provides one centimeter of water. Compare centimeters of snow per centimeter of rain for different snow and sleet storms.

People often say that 10 inches of snow will produce one inch of water. This is a rough approximation that is not always true. When the snow is dry and fluffy, it might take 15 or more inches of snow to make an inch of water. Other times, the snow may be wet and heavy, perfect for making snowmen. With slushy snow, 3 to 4 inches might be enough to melt into an inch of water. That is why you need to measure snow depth in terms of rainfall.

Experiment 1.4

Other Instruments for Your Weather Station

Materials

- ✓ **an adult**
- ✓ outdoor thermometer
- ✓ drinking straw
- ✓ large pin, such as a T-pin
- ✓ drinking glass
- ✓ water
- ✓ metallic one-gallon can with screw cap or solid rubber stopper that fits can's opening (empty olive oil can works well)
- ✓ index card
- ✓ a sink
- ✓ hot plate or stove
- ✓ hot pad or oven mitt
- ✓ sheet of cardboard
- ✓ glove
- ✓ dishpan
- ✓ tall vase or other tall vessel
- ✓ aneroid barometer

TEMPERATURE

You will need a thermometer to measure temperatures. You may already have an outdoor thermometer. If not, you can buy one at a hardware store. Air temperature readings should be made in the shade. A thermometer in the sun will show a temperature higher than the true temperature of the air.

AIR PRESSURE

We live at the bottom of an "ocean" of air. Air weighs more than you think; the air in your school classroom probably weighs between 180 and 320 kilograms (400 and 700 pounds), depending upon the room's size. It is the weight of the air in the atmosphere above you that causes air pressure. You are not aware of atmospheric pressure because it pushes on you in every direction.

The force caused by air's weight becomes evident when there is a space without air—a vacuum. When you drink with a straw, you create a partial vacuum inside your mouth. Air pressure pushes the liquid up the straw into your mouth.

What do you think will happen if you use a straw that has a hole near the top of it? To find out, use a large pin, such as a T-pin, to make a hole through the straw about two inches below the top. The hole should be between your mouth and the top of the liquid, as shown in Figure 4a.

Put the straw in a glass of water. Now try to drink through the straw. Can you explain what happens?

Place another straw in a glass of water. Put your finger firmly against the top of the straw, as shown in Figure 4b. You will find that you can use the straw to lift water from the glass. What happens when you remove your finger from the top of the straw? Can you explain why it happens?

a)

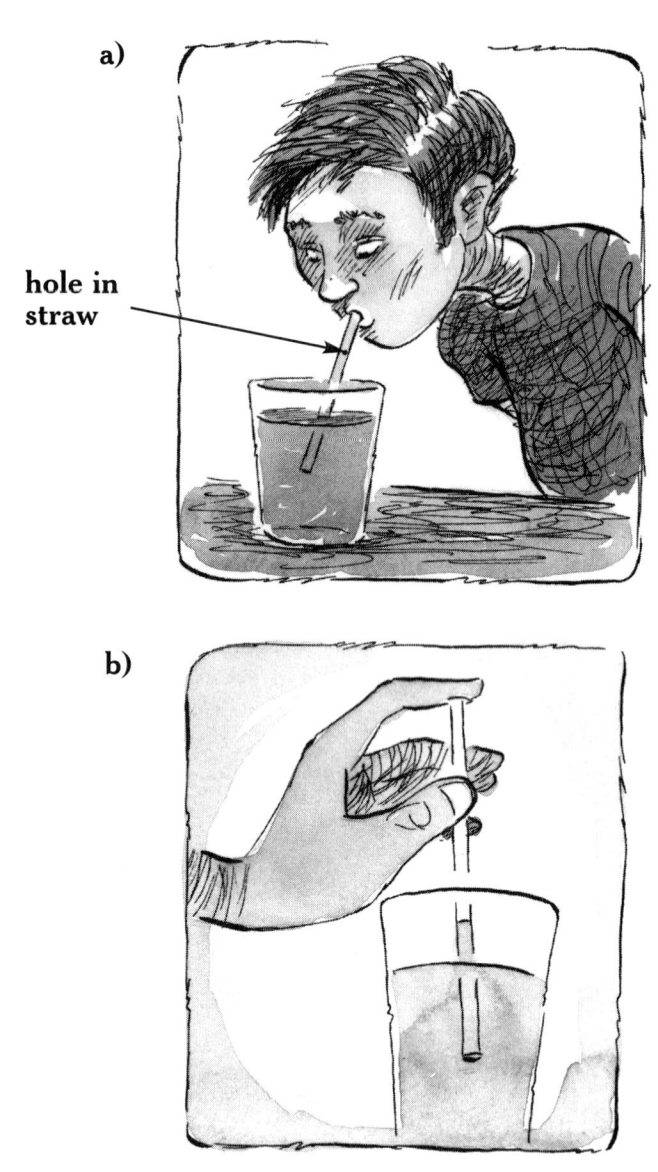

hole in straw

b)

Figure 4.

a) What happens when you try to drink through a straw that has a hole in it? b) Can you lift and transport water with a drinking straw?

Weather Maps and Instruments

To see a dramatic effect of air pressure, fill a glass with water. Place an index card over the top of the glass. Hold the card against the glass with one hand and hold the glass with the other. Continue to hold the card against the glass as you turn the glass upside down over a sink. Remove your hand from the card. Why do you think the water remains in the glass?

To see an even more dramatic effect of air pressure, pour about half a cup of water into a metallic one-gallon can. Leave the cap off. **Ask an adult** to place the can on a hot plate or stove and to turn on the hot plate. Once the water begins to boil, steam will replace the air in the can. After the water has boiled for several minutes, **ask an adult** to use a hot pad to remove the can and put it on a sheet of cardboard. **Ask an adult** to immediately use a gloved hand to screw the cap on tightly or insert a solid rubber stopper into the opening. Watch the can as the steam inside cools and changes back to a few drops of water (condenses). The can will seem to be slowly and mysteriously crushed. Can you explain why?

A BAROMETER TO MEASURE AIR PRESSURE

The first barometer—the instrument that measures air pressure—was invented by Italian scientist Evangelista Torricelli in 1643. His barometer was a tube filled with liquid mercury. Torricelli carefully covered the open end of the tube with his finger and inverted the tube into a small bowl of mercury. When he removed his finger, the mercury level fell until it was about 76 cm (30 in) above the mercury in the bowl, as shown in Figure 5. Torricelli reasoned that the space above the mercury in the tube must be a vacuum. He also reasoned that the 76-cm-high mercury column was supported by the pressure of the air on the mercury in the bowl. If he had used water in his barometer, the tube would have had to have been over 10 meters (34 feet) tall. Since mercury weighs 14 times as much as an equal volume of water, air pressure can support a column of water 14 times as high as a mercury column.

Atmospheric pressure—measured by a barometer—is also called barometric pressure.

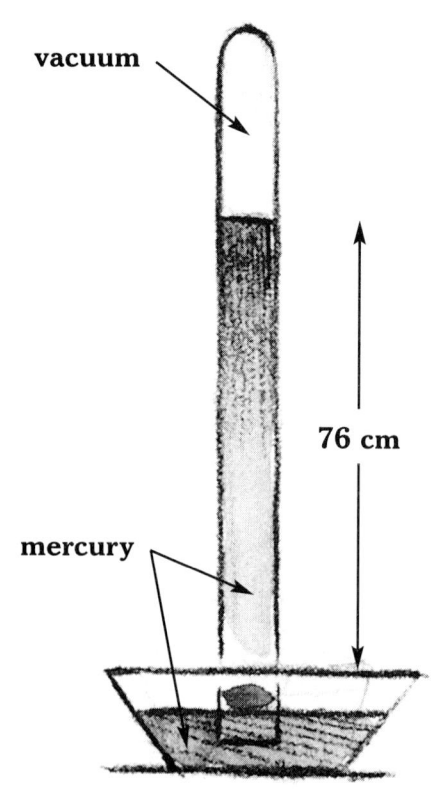

Because mercury is poisonous, you should not build a mercury barometer such as the one shown in Figure 5. However, you can show that

Figure 5.

A column of air extending to the top of the atmosphere will support a column of mercury 76 cm (30 in) high. The pressure of the mercury column equals the pressure of the air. At sea level, this pressure is normally 1.03 kilograms per square centimeter or 14.7 pounds per square inch.

Weather Maps and Instruments

air pressure will support a column of water. Fill a dishpan with water. Submerge a drinking glass in the pan and fill the glass with water. Then raise the bottom of the glass above the water level. You can see that the water in the glass is well above the water level in the pan.

Ask an adult to help you with another experiment. Fill the tallest vessel you can find that is closed at one end, like a tall vase, with water. Ask the same adult to help you cover the open end of the vessel, invert it, and place the covered end under the water in the dishpan. When you remove the cover, does the water remain in the vessel?

An aneroid barometer has no liquid. It consists of an airtight, thin, metal drum from which most of the air has been pumped out (see Figure 6). A pointer is connected to the side of the drum by sensitive gears and levers. Even small changes in air pressure cause the drum to expand or shrink very slightly. The delicate linkages magnify this motion and transmit it to the pointer on a dial. Although aneroid barometers are not as accurate as mercurial barometers, they are easily moved from place to place. You can use an aneroid barometer to measure air pressure.

Perhaps there is an aneroid barometer in your house. If not, ask if you can buy one at a hardware store or from one of the science supply companies listed in the appendix. The barometer is an important instrument to have for your weather station.

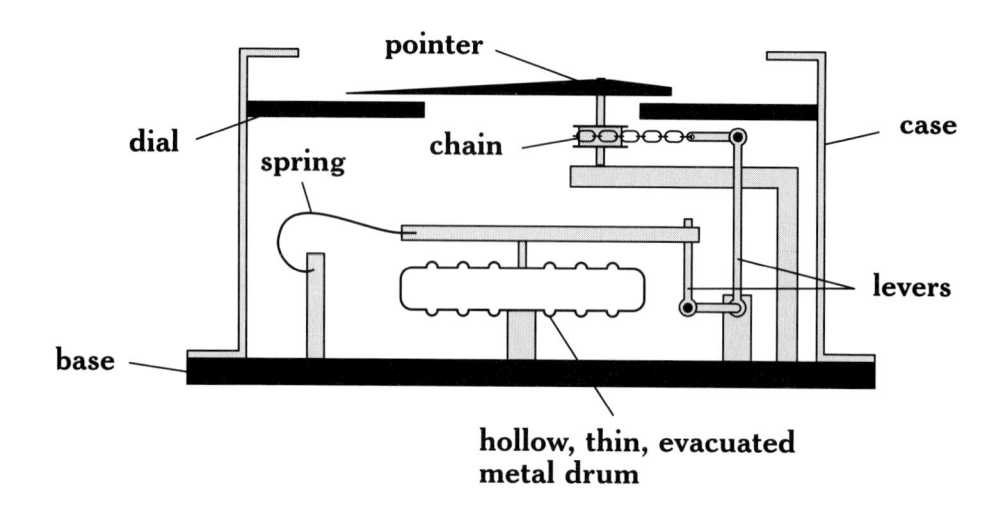

Figure 6.

An aneroid barometer is a safer way to measure air pressure than a mercury instrument.

Your barometer does not have to be outside to detect changes in air pressure. Even when all your doors and windows are tightly closed, air leaks into and out of your house, keeping the inside pressure exactly the same as the pressure outside.

Weather Maps and Instruments

Science Project Ideas

- Since water is much denser than air, a column of water exerts more pressure than a column of air of equal height. You can feel water pressure in a bucket of water. Wrap your arm inside a large plastic bag and reach into the bucket. You will be able to feel the water pushing the bag against your skin. How does the pressure change with depth in the bucket?

- Seal an aneroid barometer inside a clear plastic bag. Predict what will happen to the barometer reading as you lower the bag into a pail of water. Try it! Were you right?

- Take your barometer on an automobile trip or on an elevator. What happens to the pressure as you go up a hill or up in an elevator? What happens to the pressure as you descend a hill or go down in an elevator?

- Predict the height to which air pressure will support a column of water at sea level. Design an experiment to test your prediction. Then, **under adult supervision,** carry out your experiment.

31

Chapter 2

Earth's Atmosphere and the Sky We See

Earth is surrounded by a thin (compared to Earth's radius) blanket of air. As Figure 7 shows, meteorologists think of our atmosphere as a series of layers. Most weather takes place within the troposphere, which extends from Earth's surface to an altitude of about 13 kilometers (8 miles). As we ascend the troposphere, the temperature decreases. The tropopause is the boundary between the troposphere and the stratosphere. Temperatures in the first few miles of the stratosphere remain constant at approximately −60°C (−76°F). As we go higher, temperatures increase to nearly the freezing point of water

Earth's Atmosphere and the Sky We See

(0°C or 32°F) at the top of stratosphere. The relatively warm upper stratosphere is the result of absorption of ultraviolet light by ozone (O_3) molecules. The warm stratosphere acts as a cap on Earth's weather. It serves to create a temperature inversion

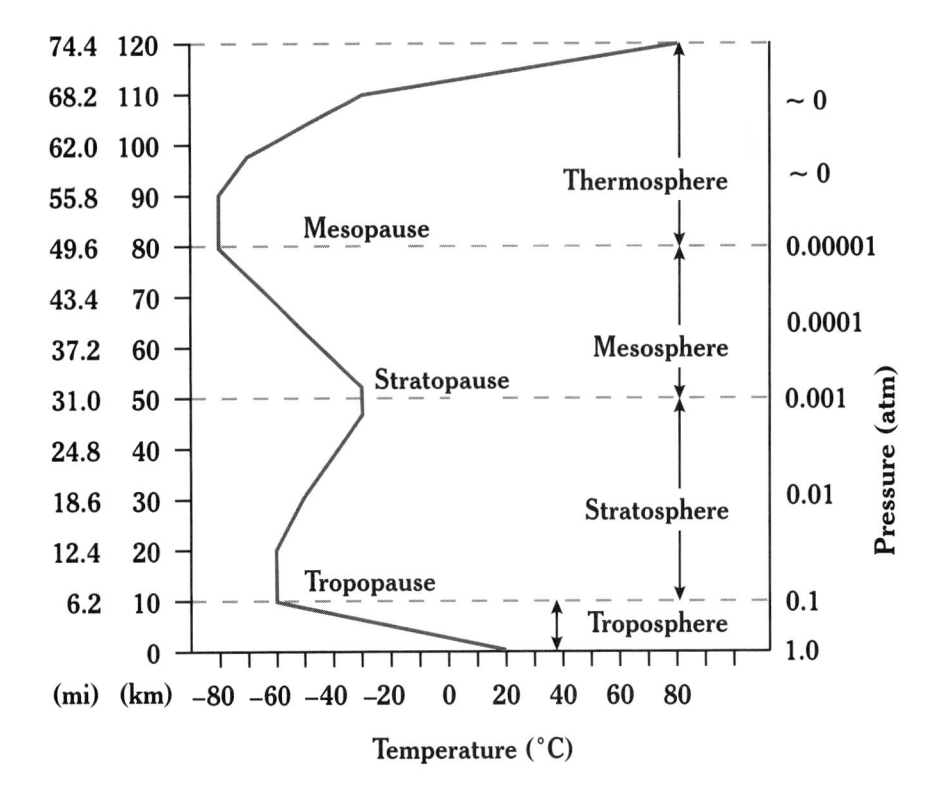

Figure 7.

This chart shows the layers of atmosphere defined by meteorologists. It also shows how pressure and temperature change at increasing altitudes.

33

(turning upside down), which, you will discover, keeps the air stable. Temperatures again diminish through the mesosphere, only to rise again in the thermosphere at altitudes greater than 80 km (50 mi).

Practically all the atmosphere's weight lies below an altitude of 100 km (60 miles). As Figure 7 reveals, air pressure at the tropopause is only one-tenth the pressure at Earth's surface. At the top of the stratosphere, the pressure is about one-thousandth its value at sea level. The density of air decreases with altitude; consequently, there is less oxygen in the air at high altitudes.

But how much of the air is oxygen? You can find out by doing the next experiment.

Experiment 2.1

What Percentage of Air Is Oxygen?

Materials

- ✓ steel wool that has no soap
- ✓ tall narrow jar (such as an olive jar) or large test tube
- ✓ vinegar
- ✓ container
- ✓ shallow dish
- ✓ water with a drop or two of food coloring
- ✓ ruler

As you probably know, iron rusts in moist air. The iron combines with oxygen to form iron oxide. Because steel wool is mostly iron, it, too, reacts with oxygen. You can therefore use steel wool to remove oxygen from air, leaving the rest, which is mostly nitrogen and a small amount of argon.

Pull a few strands of steel wool from a package of soap-free steel wool. Roll the strands into a small ball. Make several such spheres of steel wool. The balls should be slightly wider than the diameter of the narrow jar or test tube you plan to use. There is a thin coating of oil on most steel wool. To remove the oil, soak the steel wool in vinegar for about a minute. Then shake off the vinegar.

Using a pencil, push one small ball of steel wool to the bottom of a tall narrow jar or a test tube. Turn the tube or jar upside down and place it in a shallow dish of colored water (see Figure 8). Be sure the mouth of the jar is covered with water.

Leave the jar or test tube in place overnight, but observe it every few hours to see what is happening. Why do you think the water level in the jar rises as the steel wool reacts with the oxygen in the air? When the water stops rising in the jar, use a ruler to measure the total height of the jar and the height of the water in the jar. What fraction of the air originally in the jar reacted with the steel wool? Look at the steel wool. What evidence do you have that the steel wool has reacted chemically with the oxygen that was in the tube?

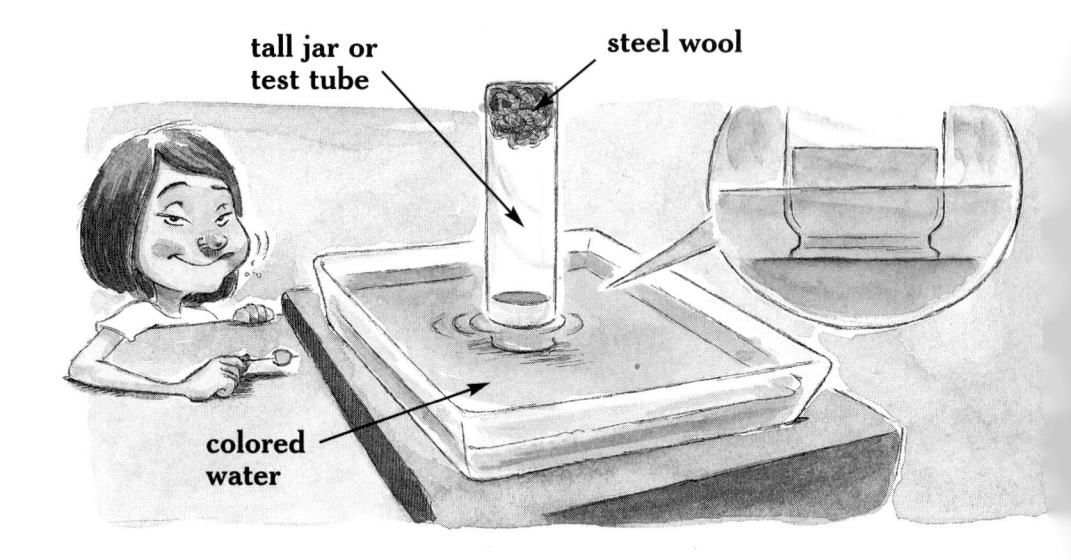

Figure 8.
Use simple materials to find what percentage of air is oxygen.

Suppose the jar is 15 cm tall and water rises 3 cm to replace the oxygen that combines with the steel wool. Then the portion of the air that was oxygen is

$$3 \text{ cm} \div 15 \text{ cm} = 1/5 \text{ or } 20\%$$

Repeat the experiment several times. Are the results consistent? Based on your experiment, what percentage of the air is oxygen?

Science Project Ideas

* You may have heard that you can find what fraction of air is oxygen by burning a candle in a jar of air inverted in water. Using the same jar, dish, and water used in Experiment 2.1, try it. Support a birthday candle with a small lump of clay, as shown in Figure 9. **Ask an adult** to light the candle. Then invert the jar over the candle. Repeat the experiment several times. Why are the results not consistent?

    If you have trouble explaining the lack of consistency, add a few drops of detergent to the water before the candle is lit. How does this help you explain the inconsistent results?

* When a candle burns, it combines with the oxygen in the air. If you place a jar of air over a burning candle, the candle will go out after a short time. But how long will it burn? To find out, support a candle with a small piece of clay. Then **ask an adult** to help you light the candle and cover it with a jar of air. How long does the candle continue to burn? If you use a bigger jar, do you predict that the candle will burn for a longer time? For less time? Or

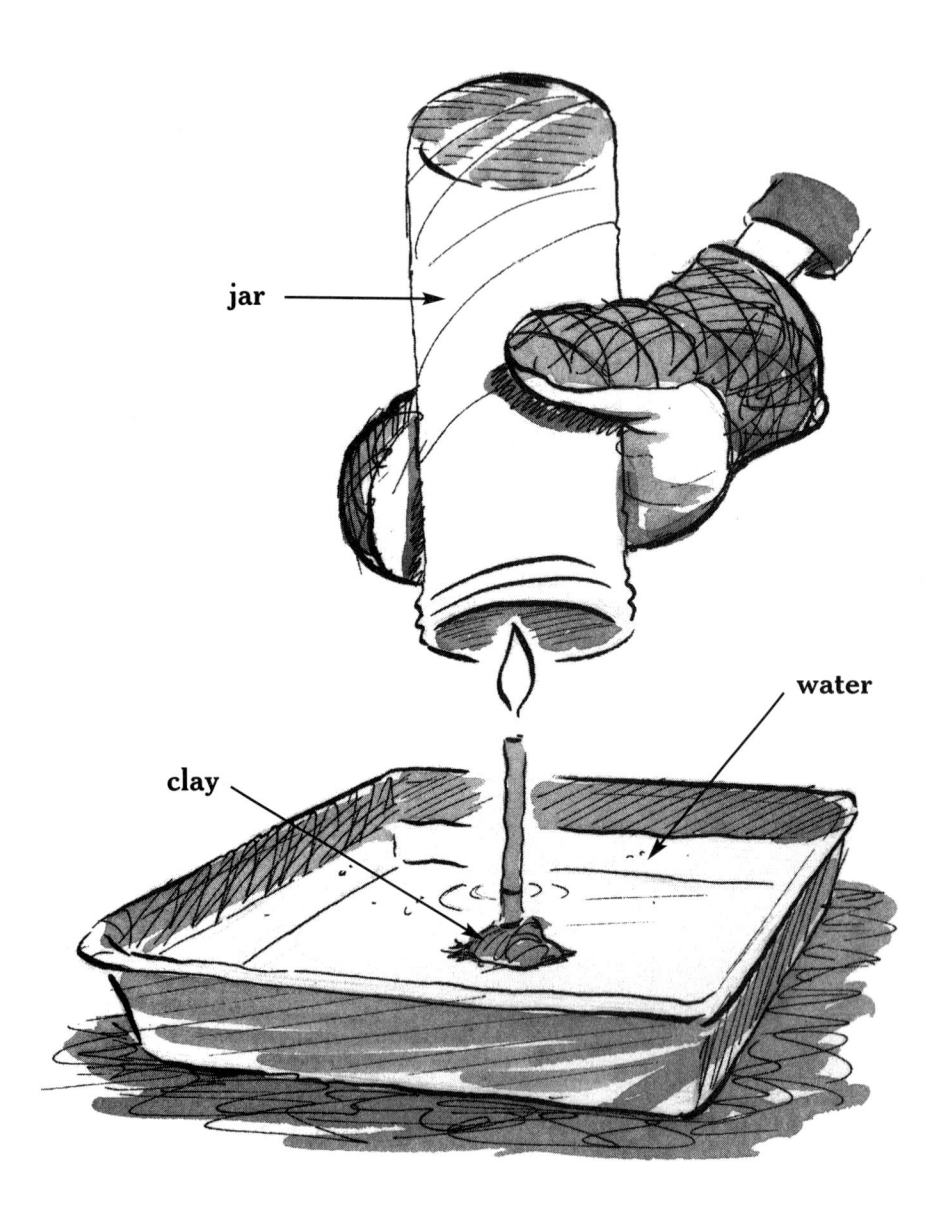

Figure 9.

Can the percentage of oxygen in air be found by burning a candle in a container inverted over water?

for the same time? How about a smaller jar? **Ask an adult to help you test your predictions.**

Now, **with adult help**, repeat Experiment 2.1 once more. Push a small ball of steel wool that has been rinsed with vinegar to the bottom of the tall, narrow jar or test tube before it is inverted over a burning candle. When the candle goes out and water stops rising in the jar, mark the water level on the jar with a marking pen or a piece of tape. Watch the water level over the next 24 hours. How can you explain the rise in the water level? Look closely at the steel wool. Is there evidence that it has reacted? Did the candle use up all of the oxygen in the jar when it burned? If not, can you figure out what fraction of the oxygen reacted with the candle?

AIR AND SKY

As you have seen, oxygen makes up about one-fifth of air. Dry air is 21 percent oxygen; 78 percent nitrogen, a relatively unreactive gas; and 1 percent argon, an inert gas. There are also small amounts of other gases such as carbon dioxide (CO_2), methane (CH_4), sulfur dioxide (SO_2), and oxides of nitrogen. The amount of water vapor in air varies with the humidity. The atmosphere also contains vast numbers of tiny solid and liquid particles (aerosols) such as smoke, soil blown into the air, and salts formed when droplets of seawater evaporate. Also present are volcanic ash and droplets of sulfuric and nitric acids formed when sulfur dioxide and oxides of nitrogen react with water vapor in the air.

It is the molecules of air and aerosols that account for the beautiful blue sky we see on a clear day. The next experiment will help you to see why the sky is blue and why sunsets are often red.

Experiment 2.2

Blue Sky, Yellow Sun, and Red Sunsets

Materials

- ✓ clear drinking glass with water
- ✓ a friend
- ✓ frosted lightbulb and lamp or socket
- ✓ powdered nondairy creamer
- ✓ spoon

Light comes to us from the sun. To reach Earth, sunlight must pass through the miles-thick atmosphere. Molecules of air and tiny aerosol particles absorb some of the sunlight that strikes them. These particles then release the "captured" light, not just in the direction the light was going, but in all directions. Because the light emitted by these particles is sent out in all directions, we say the light is scattered.

Earth's Atmosphere and the Sky We See

The scattering of sunlight by atmospheric particles has the same effect as if many tiny lightbulbs spread through the atmosphere were emitting light in all directions. Because there are so many particles and molecules in air, the sky is filled with scattered sunlight. But these lights are *not* tiny suns. The sun emits white light—a mixture of all the colors in a rainbow.

The particles in air scatter mostly blue and violet light, which have shorter wavelengths than light of other colors. Very little of the light with longer wavelengths, such as red light, is scattered. As a result, the particles act like vast numbers of tiny blue bulbs filling the sky with blue light. Above the atmosphere, where astronauts travel, the sky is black. The molecules there are so scarce that very little light is scattered. Astronauts who were on the moon reported that the moon's sky is black. What does that tell you about the moon's atmosphere?

You can make an artificial atmosphere that will scatter light. Fill a clear drinking glass with water. The water will serve as the "atmosphere." Have a friend hold the glass about a meter (yard) from a bright frosted lightbulb. The light coming through the water-filled glass represents sunlight coming through a very clear atmosphere. Look at the light from the side of the glass. Can you see any scattered light? That is, is any of the light traveling through the water scattered to your eyes?

Now look at the color of the "sun" (lightbulb) by looking through the "atmosphere" (water) from the side of the glass opposite the bulb. What is the color of the "sun" as seen through this clear atmosphere?

To scatter some light, add to the glass of water a small amount of powdered nondairy creamer. Stir the powder into the water with a spoon. Then look at the atmosphere or sky from the side of the glass again. Notice that the color of the "sky" has become slightly blue as shorter wavelengths are scattered. Look again through the "atmosphere" toward the "sun." What is the color of the "sun" now?

Continue to add more powdered nondairy creamer in small amounts. Check the model sun and sky after each addition. What happens to the color of the sky? To the color of the sun? Can you produce a red "sunset"?

Science Project Ideas

- ☀ Sometimes, when the moon rises, it is orange or bright yellow, rather than its usual pale yellow. What do you think causes this difference in color? Would you expect to see such a moon more frequently during one season than another? If so, when would you think it more likely to occur? Why?

- ☀ How could you use a fish tank and light from a slide projector to show your classmates a blue "sky" and a red "sunset"?

Earth's Atmosphere and the Sky We See

Experiment 2.3

Rainbows in the Sky and Elsewhere

Materials

- ✓ bright sunlight
- ✓ water hose with spray nozzle
- ✓ clear, rectangular, plastic container
- ✓ window with bright sunlight
- ✓ mirror
- ✓ white paper
- ✓ cardboard
- ✓ tape

Blue skies and red sunsets are not the only colors you find in the atmosphere. Sometimes the sky is filled with a rainbow. As the English poet William Wordsworth once wrote:

My heart leaps up when I behold
A rainbow in the sky.

You can make a rainbow of your own with some very simple materials. The simplest one, the one closest to the formation of a natural rainbow, can be made by spraying water in sunlight. On a sunny day, stand with your back to the sun. Hold the nozzle of a hose in front of you and spray a fine mist into the air. You should be able to see a rainbow in the tiny, closely spaced drops of water.

43

You can also make a less natural rainbow inside even when water is frozen outside. To make this rainbow, nearly fill a clear, rectangular, plastic container with water. Put the water near a bright window where sunlight can strike the water straight on. Place a mirror in the water at an angle to the water's surface, as shown in Figure 10. Light passing through the water will be reflected by the mirror and emerge from the water's surface. Move a sheet of white paper taped to a piece of cardboard into the reflected light. You will see a bright patch of reflected white light. Continue to move the cardboard and paper and look closely. You will find a less bright band of colors stretching from red to violet, the same colors found in a rainbow. In the next experiment you will find out how these colors are produced.

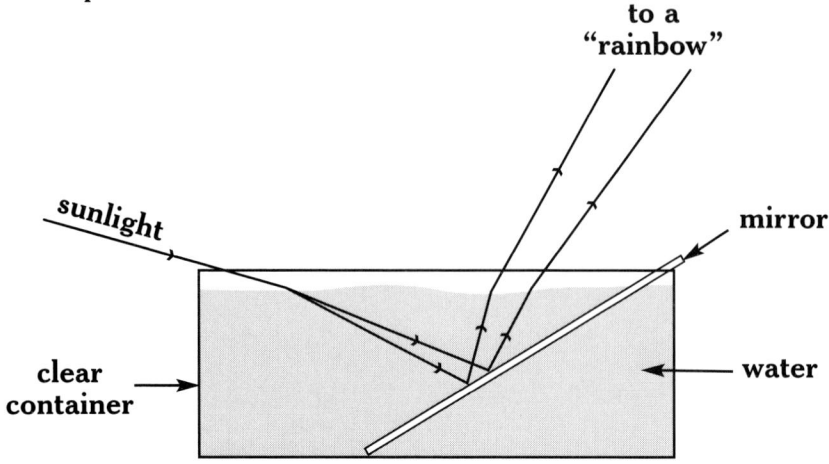

Figure 10.

You can make a "rainbow" by reflecting sunlight from a mirror placed in water.

Earth's Atmosphere and the Sky We See

Experiment 2.4

Bending Light to Make a "Rainbow"

Materials

- ✓ dark room
- ✓ clear drinking glass
- ✓ water
- ✓ sheet of heavy black construction paper
- ✓ flashlight
- ✓ ruler
- ✓ scissors
- ✓ clear, rectangular, plastic container

You can carry out several experiments that will help you understand how a rainbow is made. To begin, you will need a dark room and a clear drinking glass filled with water. Shine a flashlight into the water. Move the light around to different positions. You will see that some of the reflected light contains a mixture of colors like those in a rainbow.

To see what happens more clearly, build a "ray maker" from a 7.5 cm × 10 cm (3 in × 4 in) piece of heavy black construction paper. With scissors, cut a narrow slit, 2 cm ($1/16$ in) wide, in the center of the paper as shown in Figure 11a. Fold the ends of the paper so that it will stand upright.

Nearly fill a clear, rectangular, plastic container with water. Arrange the container, ray maker, and flashlight so that the light beam strikes the water at an angle as shown in Figure 11b.

Darken the room, then use the ray maker and a strong flashlight to produce a narrow beam of light as shown. You can see the light bend at the point where it enters the water. It is bent again as it leaves the water.

The bending of light as it passes from one substance to another is called refraction. In this experiment, the light bends as it passes from air to water, and again when it passes from water to air. As you may know, a triangular-shaped glass, called a prism, can also be used to refract light and create a rainbow. With a little patience, you can do the same thing with the materials used in this experiment.

Arrange the ray maker and flashlight so that the light enters the water at a very small angle between the light ray and the water (see Figure 11c). The corner of the container will then act like a triangular water prism and produce a rainbow. (Save the ray maker for other experiments.)

Once you have made the rainbow, you can see that different colors of light are refracted slightly more or less than others. Which color is bent the most? Which color is bent the least? The separation of white light into colors as a result of their being bent more or less is called dispersion.

The formation of a natural rainbow is quite complicated. However, the basic explanation is shown in Figure 12. Sunlight enters raindrops, where it is refracted, causing some dispersion. The light is reflected (at B in Figure 12a) and refracted again as it leaves the drops, causing more dispersion.

Earth's Atmosphere and the Sky We See

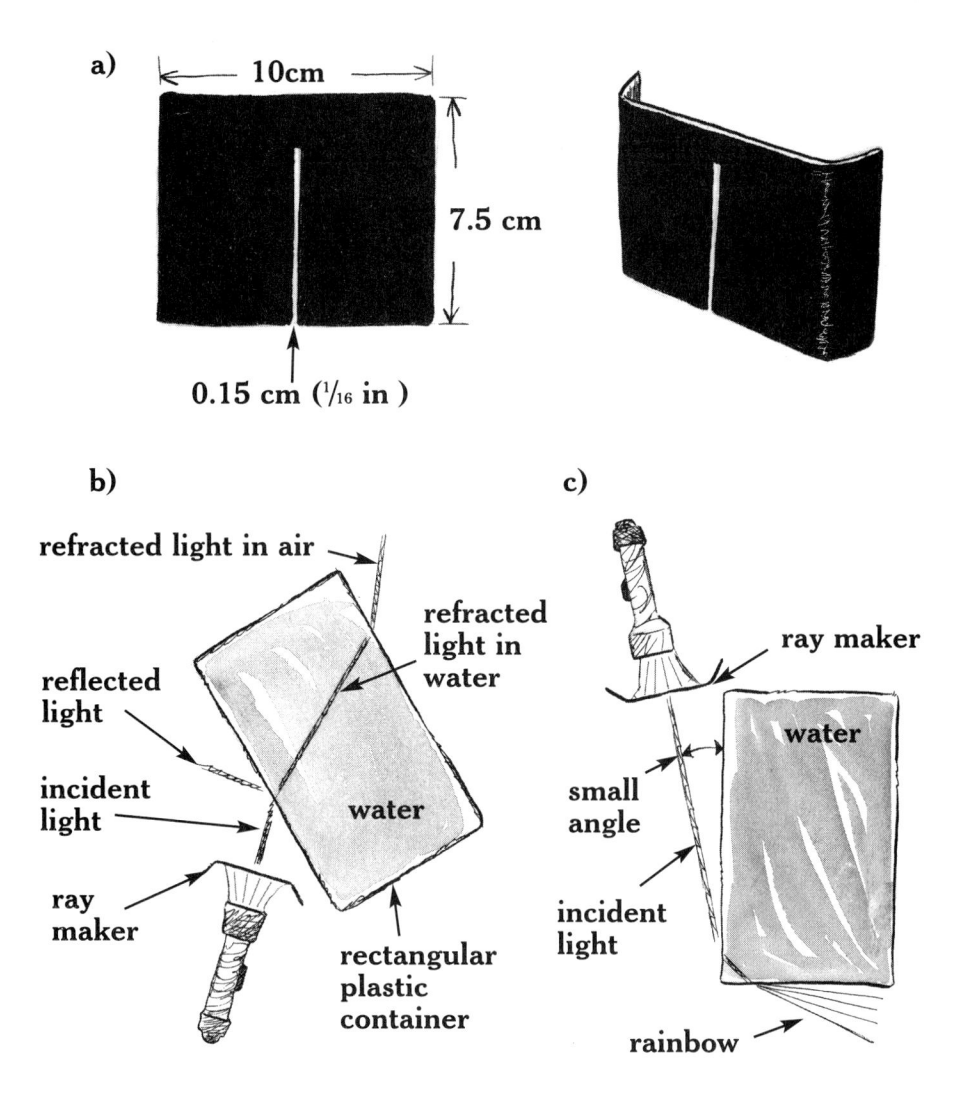

Figure 11.
a) A ray maker can be prepared from a piece of heavy black construction paper. b) An overhead view of light being refracted by water. c) An overhead view of light being refracted by water at a small angle from the water. The water in the corner of the container acts like a prism, producing a "rainbow."

As you can see, red light will be at the base of the rainbow and violet at the top. Some light, as shown in Figure 12b, is reflected twice, giving rise to a second rainbow in which the arrangement of colors is reversed.

The primary and brightest rainbow will appear at an angle of about 42 degrees from your eyes. If a secondary rainbow is visible, it will be at an angle of about 51 degrees (see Figure 12c).

Occasionally, you will see rainbows when sunlight, searchlights, or car headlights reflect off tiny fog droplets. You might also find rainbows on dew-covered grass illuminated by morning sunlight, or on trees illuminated by the sun after an ice storm. Rainbows, or partial rainbows, sometimes appear when you least expect them. Look for them! And when you see them, try to figure out for yourself why they are there.

Science Project Ideas

- From what you have read and observed, what conditions are necessary for a rainbow to appear in the sky?
- You usually see a rainbow as a semicircular arc. From where might you see a circular rainbow?
- Design and carry out an experiment to measure the angles that primary and secondary rainbows make with your eyes.

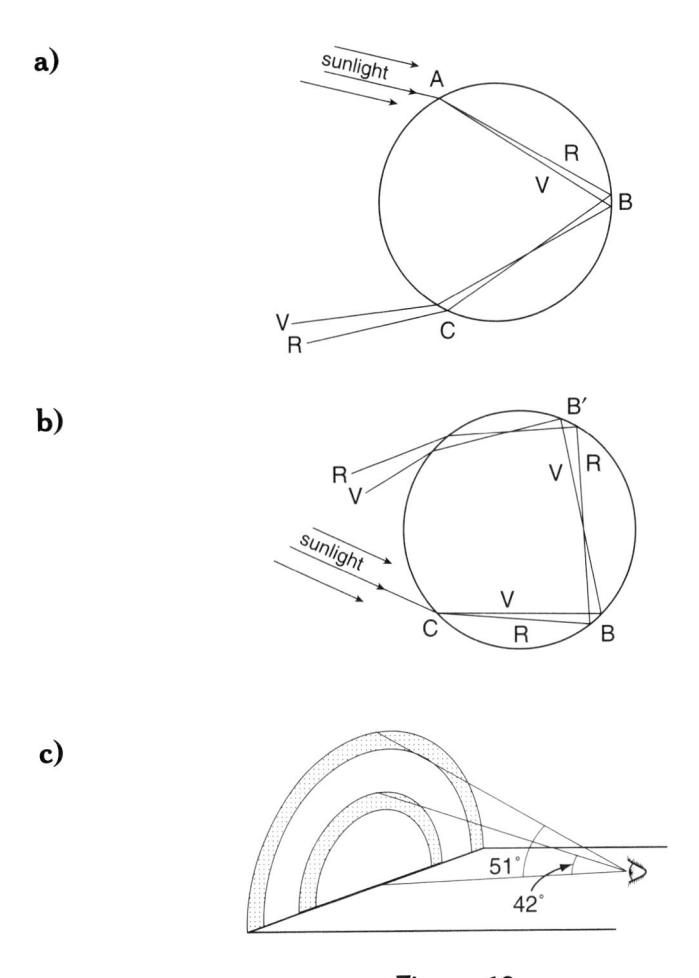

Figure 12.

Sunlight entering a raindrop is refracted and reflected. The different colors in white light are refracted by different amounts, causing the colors to separate (disperse).
a) Sunlight refracted at A is reflected at B, then refracted again at C as it leaves the drop. Such drops cause the primary rainbow (V = violet light; R = red light). b) A secondary rainbow is produced by drops that reflect sunlight twice, at B and B'.
c) Primary and secondary rainbows form at 42 and 51 degree angles, respectively.

Experiment 2.5

Refraction at Sunrise, Sunset, and in a Cup

Materials

- ✓ coin
- teacup
- partner
- water

Because of refraction, you can see the sun while it is below the horizon at sunrise and sunset. In the space between Earth and the sun, there is a virtual vacuum. When light enters Earth's atmosphere, it is bent more and more as the atmosphere's density increases (see Figure 13a). As a result, the sun appears to be at a higher level than it actually is.

You can see a similar effect in your own home. Place a coin on the bottom of a teacup. Stand several feet from the cup and lower your head until the coin disappears from your view. Have a partner slowly add water to the cup without disturbing the coin. Suddenly, without raising your head, you will be able to see the coin. Can you explain why? (See Figure 13b.)

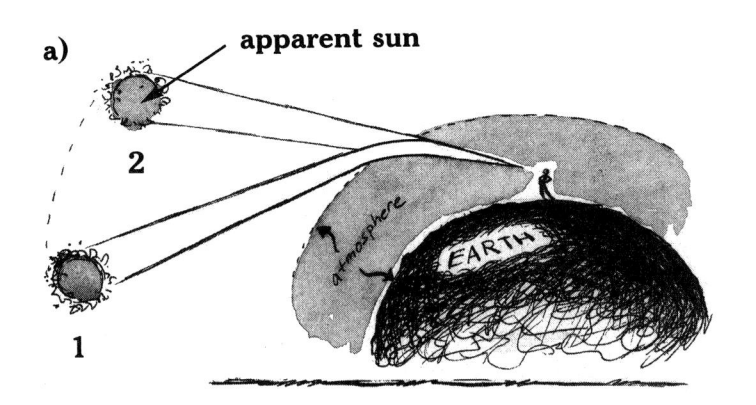

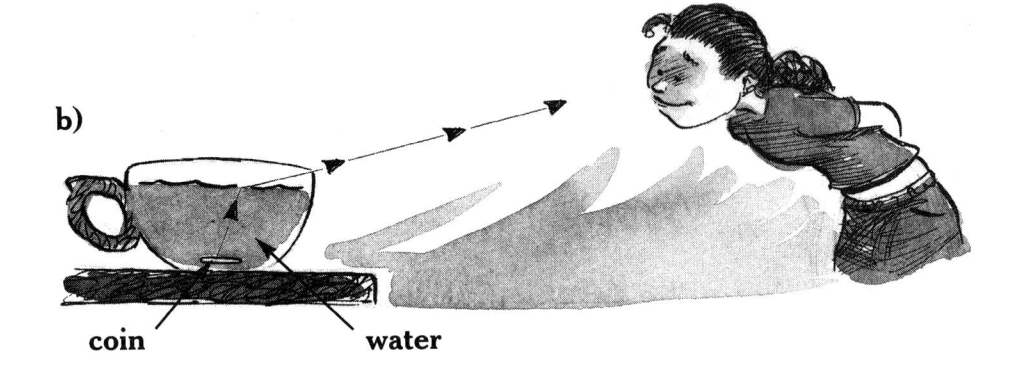

Earth's Atmosphere and the Sky We See

Figure 13.
a) Refraction of sunlight makes the sun appear to be higher in the sky than it actually is. The actual position is at 1; the apparent position is at 2. b) A similar effect can make a coin appear when water is added to the cup, causing light to refract as it leaves the water.

Chapter 3

Humidity, Sunshine, and Weather

When water evaporates, it becomes a gas or vapor and mixes with the air. Humidity is a measure of the amount of water vapor in the air. There is a limit to the quantity of water vapor air can hold, but the warmer the air, the more moisture it can hold. When air holds the maximum amount of water possible for a particular temperature, we say the air is saturated with moisture. The dew point is the temperature at which air is or would be saturated with water vapor. At the dew point, moisture in the air begins to condense—to form water droplets.

Generally, air temperature and dew point are the same when it is raining. Dry air will have a very low dew point. For

Humidity, Sunshine, and Weather

example, dry air at a temperature of 80°F might have a dew point of 40°F. Such air would have to be cooled forty degrees before moisture in that air would begin to condense. Any perspiration that might form on your body would quickly evaporate, producing a cooling effect on your skin. On the other hand, if the dew point of air is 78°F, the air holds lots of water. The air would feel uncomfortably damp. You would probably say it was muggy or very humid.

Table 2 reveals that the warmer the air, the more water vapor it can hold.

Table 2.
THE MAXIMUM AMOUNT OF WATER VAPOR THAT CAN BE FOUND IN A CUBIC METER OF AIR AT DIFFERENT TEMPERATURES.

Air Temperature (°C)	(°F)	Grams of water per m^3
0	32	4.8
5	41	6.8
10	50	9.3
15	59	12.7
20	68	17.1
25	77	22.8
30	86	30.0
35	95	39.2

Relative humidity is the amount of water vapor the air holds at a certain temperature compared with the total amount it could hold at that temperature. For example, when the relative humidity is 50 percent, it means the air contains half of the moisture it could hold at its present temperature. When the relative humidity is 100 percent, the air contains the maximum amount of water vapor it can hold.

Relative humidity usually changes during the day as the air temperature changes from sunrise to sunset. Yet the actual amount of vapor in the air may remain about the same. In the morning, when the air is cooler, the relative humidity might be 75 percent. As the air warms, the relative humidity of the same air could drop to 60 percent by noon.

You will often find dew on grass and flowers after a cool, clear night. Why is dew less likely to form if clouds fill the sky?

Experiment 3.1

Finding the Dew Point

Materials

- ✓ shiny metal can
- ✓ thermometer
- ✓ ice
- ✓ warm water

Unless it is raining, the amount of moisture in the air is usually less than the maximum quantity it can hold. The dampness of

Humidity, Sunshine, and Weather

air can be measured by the absolute humidity—the quantity of water vapor in one cubic meter of air. Absolute humidity is determined by finding the dew point of the air—the temperature at which dew begins to form. For example, if the temperature of the air is 20°C (68°F), it can hold a maximum of 17.1 g/m^3, as shown in Table 2.

If you slowly lower the temperature of some water in a shiny metal can, you can find the temperature at which dew begins to collect on the can's outside surface. The temperature of the air touching the can will quickly acquire the temperature of the can and the water in it. When the temperature in the can reaches the temperature at which the air is saturated with water vapor, moisture will begin to collect on the can's surface.

Suppose dew appears when the water and can are at 10°C (50°F). We then know that the air touching the can contains 9.3 g/m^3—the maximum amount of water vapor air can hold at 10°C (see Table 2).

The *absolute* humidity of this air would be 9.3 g/m^3; that is, 9.3 grams of water per cubic meter of air. The *relative* humidity of air is the ratio of the quantity of water vapor the air *does* hold to the quantity it *could* hold if it were saturated with moisture. If the air temperature is 20°C (68°F), the air could hold 17.1 g/m^3. Consequently, the relative humidity of the air is 9.3 ÷ 17.1 (0.54), or 54 percent.

To find the dew point and absolute humidity of the air in or outside your home or school, pour some warm water into a shiny metal can. Stir the water carefully with a thermometer as you lower the water temperature by adding small pieces of ice. Watch the surface of the can closely. When dew droplets are seen on the can's surface, note the temperature of the water. You have reached the dew point of the air. Why can you assume that the water, can, and air touching the can are all at the same temperature?

Use your experimental data and Table 2 to determine the absolute humidity of the air.

Figure 14 is a graph of the data in Table 2. The graph will help you determine values for humidity at temperatures not given in the table.

What is the relative humidity of the air in your experiment? How does the humidity outside the building compare with the humidity inside?

Use the same apparatus, table, and graph to determine the dew point and humidity (absolute and relative) on clear, cloudy, and rainy days, and at different times of the year. Record your findings. During which season of the year does the absolute humidity tend to be highest? Lowest? When is the relative humidity highest? Lowest? During which season of the year is the air driest inside your home or school? Under what conditions are you unable to determine the dew point?

Humidity, Sunshine, and Weather

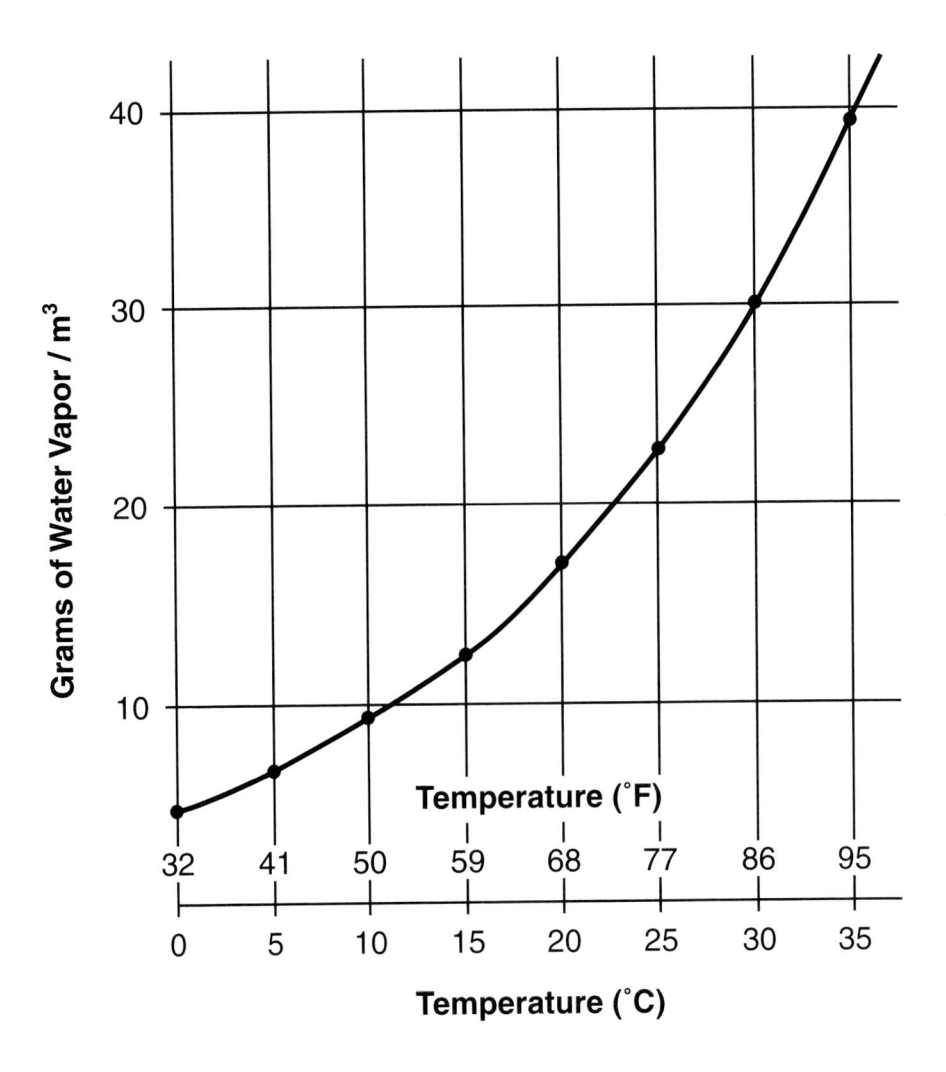

Figure 14.

This graph shows the maximum amount of water in a cubic meter of air at various temperatures.

Science Project Ideas

* Design and carry out an experiment to show why you should use a metal rather than a plastic or glass container to find the dew point.

* Do some research to find out how the data in Table 2 was obtained.

* Fill the can you used in Experiment 3.1 about one-third of the way with crushed ice. Add an equal volume of table salt and stir to thoroughly mix the salt and ice. Place a thermometer in the salt-ice mixture. Watch the side of the can very carefully. Do you see frost collecting? Do you first see dew that freezes, or does the frost form without first becoming a liquid (dew)?

Experiment 3.2

Measuring Humidity with a Hygrometer

Materials

- ✓ 2 thermometers
- ✓ scissors
- ✓ shoelace
- ✓ empty cardboard milk carton
- ✓ rubber bands
- ✓ water
- ✓ small piece of cardboard
- ✓ small knife

An instrument called a hygrometer can be used to measure humidity. Some hygrometers are made with a human hair. An increase in humidity causes the hair's length to increase slightly and move a recording device. Such devices are rather delicate.

You will find it easier to make a hygrometer with two thermometers, one with a dry bulb and the other with a wet bulb. The dry bulb is just an ordinary thermometer. The bulb of the wet-bulb thermometer is covered with a piece of moist cloth, which cools the thermometer as the water evaporates. In dry air, the water evaporates rapidly, causing a significant temperature decrease. In humid air, evaporation occurs more slowly, and there is a smaller temperature decrease. If the humidity is 100 percent, the two thermometers will have the same reading.

To make your hygrometer, cut a piece of shoelace about 6 inches (15 cm) long. Slip the cut end over the bulb of one thermometer. Attach the thermometers to an empty milk carton with rubber bands as shown in Figure 15. Cut a hole in the carton near the lace, and push the lace through the hole so that it rests on the bottom. Then pour water into the carton. Water will ascend the lace and keep the bulb wet.

Before using the hygrometer, be sure the lace around the thermometer bulb is wet. To take a reading on your hygrometer, use a small piece of stiff cardboard to fan the wet bulb for 5 minutes. Then quickly read the temperatures on both thermometers, and record them in your notebook. Subtract the wet-bulb temperature reading from the dry-bulb reading to find the difference in the temperatures.

Use Table 3 to find the relative humidity. Find the temperature closest to the dry bulb temperature at the left side of the table. Next, find the number at the top of the table that matches the difference you found between the wet bulb and dry bulb temperatures. The percent of relative humidity is given where the dry temperature row intersects the temperature difference column. For example, if the dry-bulb temperature is 16°C (60°F) and the wet-bulb temperature is 10°C (50°F), then the relative humidity is 48 percent.

If you have a sling psychrometer (see Science Project Ideas that follow), you will find it quite easy to measure relative humidity on a daily basis.

Humidity, Sunshine, and Weather

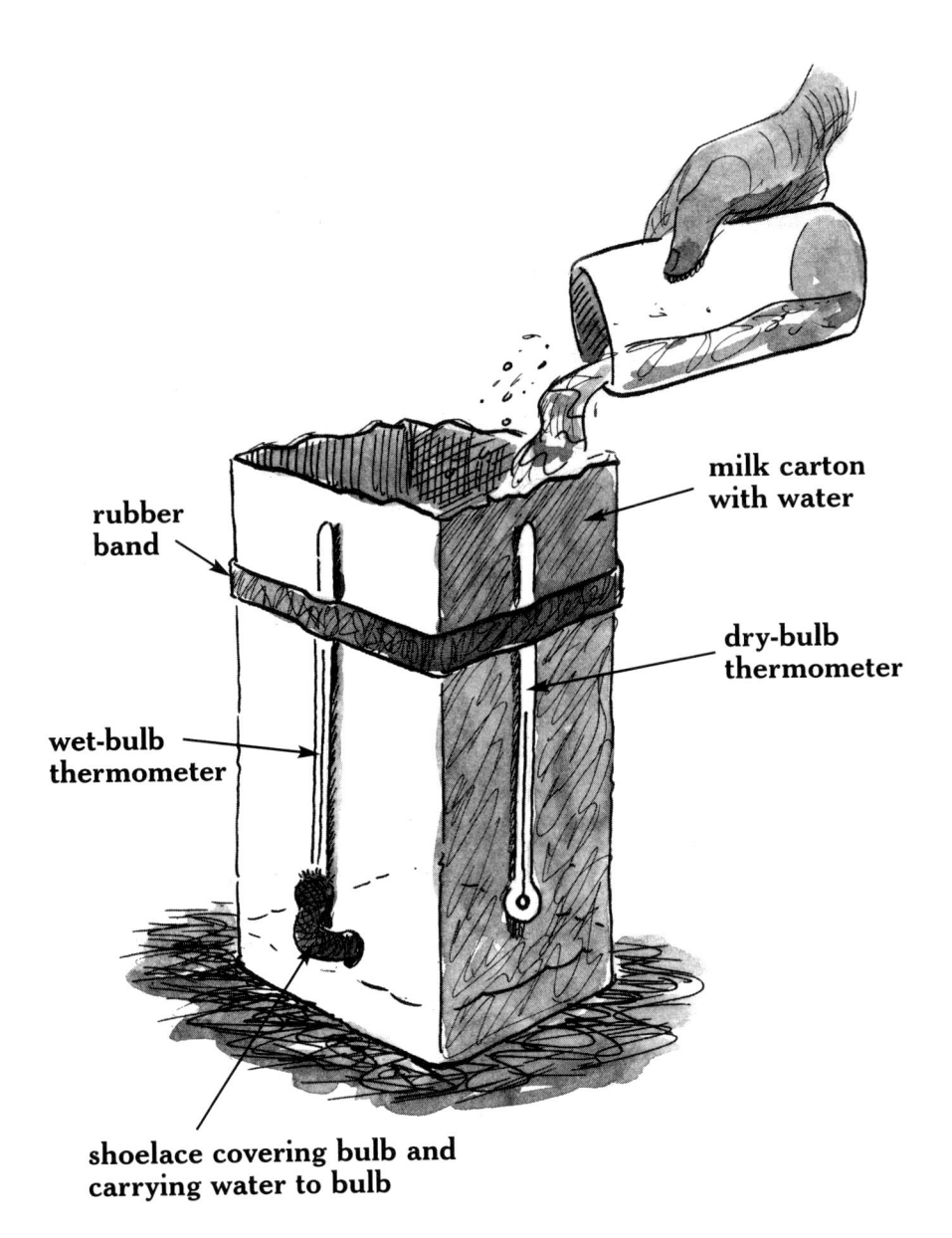

Figure 15.

You can make a hygrometer to measure relative humidity.

Table 3.
FINDING THE RELATIVE HUMIDITY (PERCENT) USING FAHRENHEIT TEMPERATURES

Dry Bulb Temp, °F	Difference in Temperature, °F (dry-bulb temp — wet-bulb temp)																			
	1	2	3	4	5	6	7	8	9	10	11	12	13	14	15	16	17	18	19	20	25
10			78	56	34	13															
15			82	64	46	29	11														
20	85	70	55	40	26	12															
25			87	74	62	49	37	25	13												
30			89	78	67	56	46	36	26	16											
35			91	81	72	63	54	45	36	27	19	10									
40			92	83	75	68	60	52	45	37	29	22	15								
45			93	86	78	71	64	57	51	44	38	31	25	18	12						
50	93	87	80	74	67	61	55	49	43	38	32	27	21	16	10						
55	94	88	82	76	70	65	59	54	49	43	38	33	28	23	19	14					
60	94	89	83	78	73	68	63	58	53	48	44	39	35	31	27	24	20	16	12		
65	95	90	85	80	75	70	66	61	56	52	48	44	39	35	31	27	24	20	16	12	
70	95	90	86	81	77	72	68	64	59	55	51	48	44	40	36	33	29	25	22	19	
75	96	91	86	82	78	74	70	66	62	58	54	51	47	44	40	37	34	30	27	24	
80	96	91	87	83	79	75	72	68	64	61	57	54	50	47	44	41	38	35	32	29	15
85	96	92	88	84	80	76	73	69	66	62	59	56	52	49	46	43	41	38	35	32	20
90	96	92	89	85	81	78	74	71	68	65	61	58	55	52	49	47	44	41	39	36	24
95	96	93	89	85	82	79	75	72	69	66	63	60	57	54	51	49	46	43	41	38	27

Humidity, Sunshine, and Weather

Science Project Ideas

- If possible, obtain a sling psychrometer from your school's science classroom. Use it to determine relative humidity. What advantages does a sling psychrometer have over the hygrometer you made?

- How can you measure dew point when it is less than water's freezing temperature of 32°F (0°C)?

HUMIDITY AND DENSITY OF AIR

People often say humid air is "heavy," suggesting that humid air is denser than dry air. In fact, just the opposite is true. As your weather records have probably shown, damp air is often accompanied by low barometric (atmospheric) pressure. Air containing water vapor is less dense than dry air, and for a very good reason.

As any chemist will tell you, equal volumes of gases at the same temperature and pressure contain equal numbers of molecules. Water molecules weigh less than oxygen, nitrogen, and argon molecules. In damp air, water molecules have taken the place of some of the oxygen, nitrogen, and argon molecules. Consequently, a volume of humid air weighs less than an equal volume of dry air.

63

Experiment 3.3

Weather Records at Your Weather Station

Materials

- ✓ weather instruments from Experiments 1.2, 1.4, and 3.2: wind vane, anemometer (wind speed), rain gauge, thermometer, barometer (air pressure), hygrometer (humidity)
- ✓ notebook
- ✓ pen or pencil

Now that you have made instruments for measuring weather, including dew points and humidity, you can begin to keep daily records. The data you collect can be kept in a notebook. Each day, as often as you can, record the date, the time, temperature, wind speed, wind direction, air pressure, rain- or snowfall, dew point, humidity, and sky conditions.

For sky conditions, you can record whether the sky is fair, partly cloudy, cloudy, or precipitating (rain or snow). Your chart might look like the one in Figure 16, which includes symbols to represent sky conditions.

You may want to compare your findings to those in a newspaper or television report.

Humidity, Sunshine, and Weather

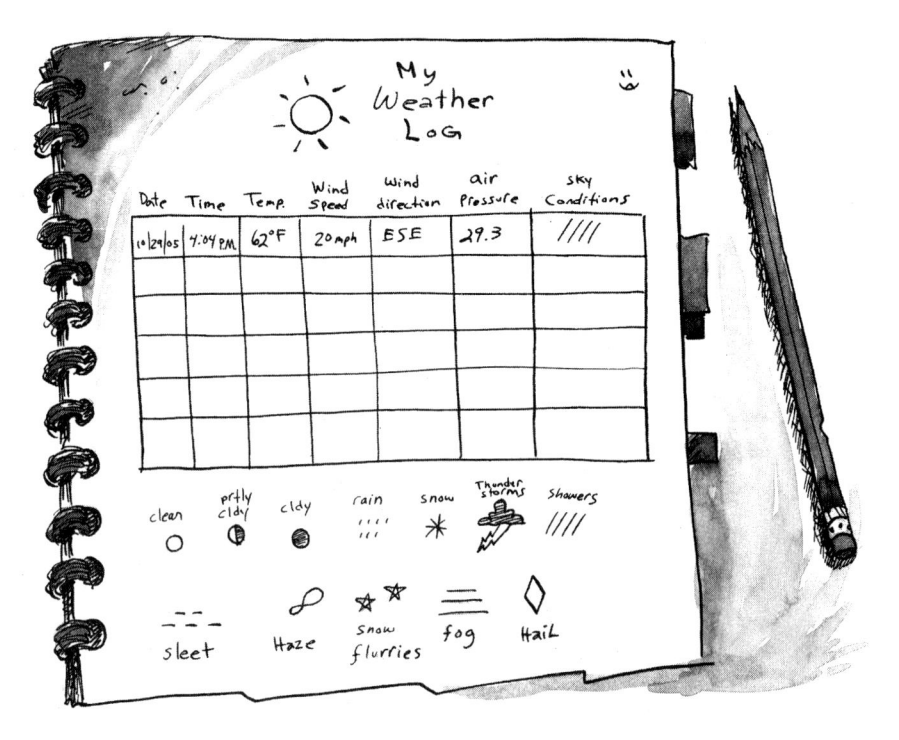

Figure 16.

A weather record containing one set of sample data.

EARTH'S SOURCE OF HEAT

The sun is Earth's major source of heat. And it is solar energy that produces Earth's ever-changing weather. There is some heat within Earth. Sometimes this heat becomes quite evident when a volcano erupts, spewing red-hot lava over the surrounding land. However, the heat within Earth is negligible compared to that delivered by the sun.

If all the solar energy falling on Earth's atmosphere reached Earth's surface, temperatures would be too high to sustain life.

Fortunately, clouds reflect much of the sun's energy back into space.

In the experiments that follow, you will see how solar energy and Earth's tilted axis relative to the sun are responsible for our seasons. You will learn how the sun's energy is stored in Earth's land and water. And you will investigate how water from Earth's surface is changed to rain.

SUN AND SEASONS

If you live at latitudes greater than 30 degrees, you experience seasonal changes in the weather. You find that average daily winter temperatures are significantly lower than those in summer. Many people believe the variation in seasonal temperatures occurs because Earth's elliptical orbit brings us closer to the sun in the summer than in the winter. But in fact, Earth's perihelion (when it is closest to the sun) occurs between January 1 and 4, when it is about 147,500,000 km (91,650,000 miles) from the sun. Earth's aphelion (when it is farthest from the sun) occurs between July 2 and 6, when it is about 152,500,000 km (94,760,000 miles) from the sun.

The real reason for seasons is the 23.5-degree tilt of Earth's axis to the plane of its orbit about the sun. Figure 17 shows Earth at four different times in its path around the sun. As you can see in Figure 17a, on December 21 (often the first day of winter in the Northern Hemisphere) the region within the Arctic Circle, from 90 degrees to 66.5 degrees

Humidity, Sunshine, and Weather

latitude, will not see the sun. Meanwhile, in a similar region around the South Pole, within the Antarctic Circle, the sun will be visible for 24 hours. The reverse is true of the two polar regions on June 21 (Figure 17c), the beginning of summer north of the equator. On March 21 (Figure 17b), the beginning of spring north of the equator, the sun will be on

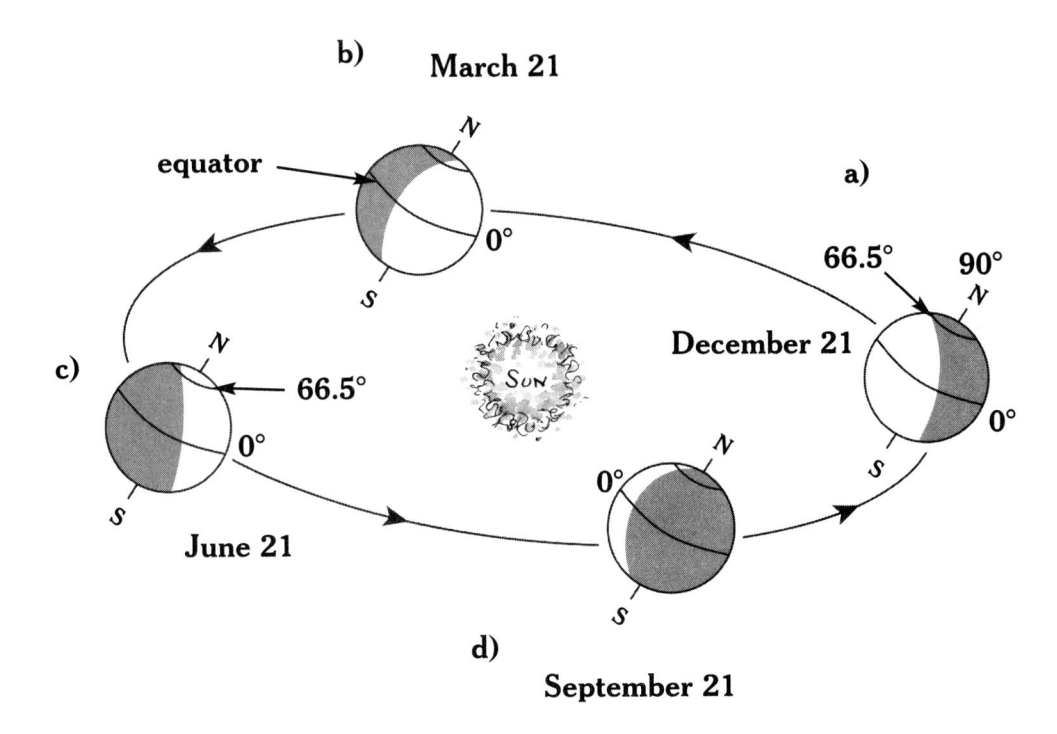

Figure 17.
Earth is shown at different times in its yearly orbit about the sun. Seasons shown are for the Northern Hemisphere.
a) winter; b) spring; c) summer; d) autumn.

the horizon at both the South and the North Pole, and it will be directly overhead on the equator. The same will be true on September 21 (Figure 17d), often the first day of autumn in the Northern Hemisphere.

Experiment 3.4

Why Is Summer Hot and Winter Cold?

Materials

- ✓ sheet of paper
- ✓ table
- ✓ flashlight
- ✓ globe
- ✓ dark room

A simple experiment will help you see why summer is so much warmer than winter. Place a sheet of paper on a table. Shine a flashlight directly onto the paper. Now, tip the flashlight so that its light strikes the paper at an angle much less than 90 degrees. What happens to the area covered by the light from the flashlight? How has the amount of light per area changed? Does the same amount of light spread out over a larger area of paper?

Place a globe on a table in a dark room. Assume it is the beginning of summer in the Southern Hemisphere (around December 21). The sun will be directly over the Tropic of

Humidity, Sunshine, and Weather

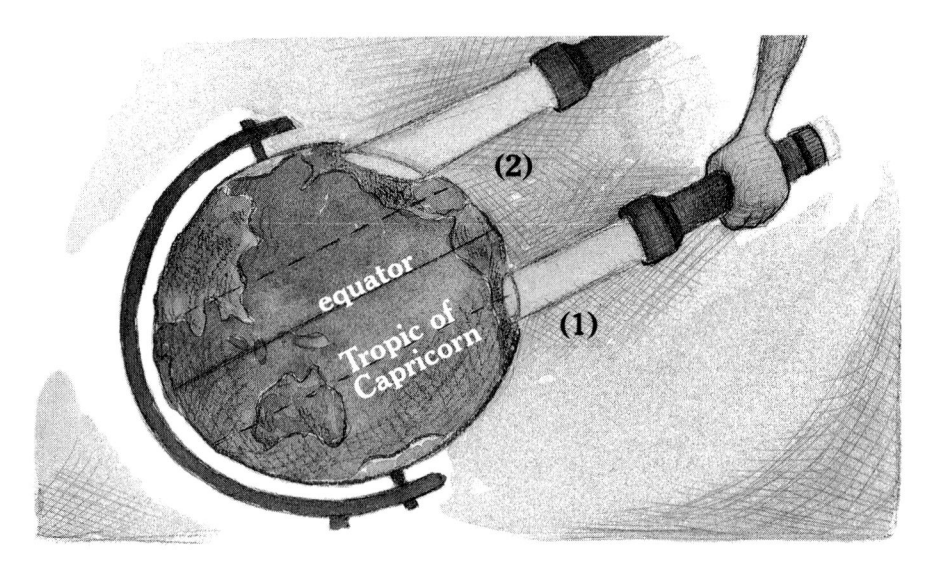

Figure 18.
Light from the "sun" shining directly on a globe's Tropic of Capricorn (1). The same "sun" shining on the globe's United States (2).

Capricorn, which you can find on the globe. Hold the flashlight directly over the line representing the Tropic of Capricorn at a point south (on the globe) of the United States as shown in Figure 18. Practically all the sun's light rays reaching Earth on this date will be parallel to those striking the Tropic of Capricorn. Slowly move the flashlight upward, keeping it tilted at the same angle, until the light shines on the United States, as represented on the globe in Figure 18. What has happened to the same amount of light shining on the globe? Does the light cover more, the same, or less area than it did when it was shining on the Tropic of Capricorn?

Sunlight is the energy that heats Earth. How will the sun's heat delivered to one square foot of United States soil compare with the heat delivered to the same area near the Tropic of Capricorn on December 21?

Experiment 3.5

The Effect of Angle on the Absorption of Radiant Energy

Materials

- ✓ 3 identical thermometers
- ✓ black construction paper
- ✓ scissors
- ✓ stapler
- ✓ ruler
- ✓ heat lamp or reflector light and clamp with 75-watt bulb
- ✓ books
- ✓ clock or watch
- ✓ notebook and pen or pencil

As you have seen, sunlight striking Earth's surface at an angle, such as 40 degrees, is spread over more area than light shining straight down on Earth at 90 degrees. When the sun is overhead, the sun's energy is concentrated on a smaller area. In this experiment you can see the effect of the sun's angle in a somewhat more direct way.

You will need three identical thermometers. For each thermometer, prepare a black pocket by cutting rectangles from

Humidity, Sunshine, and Weather

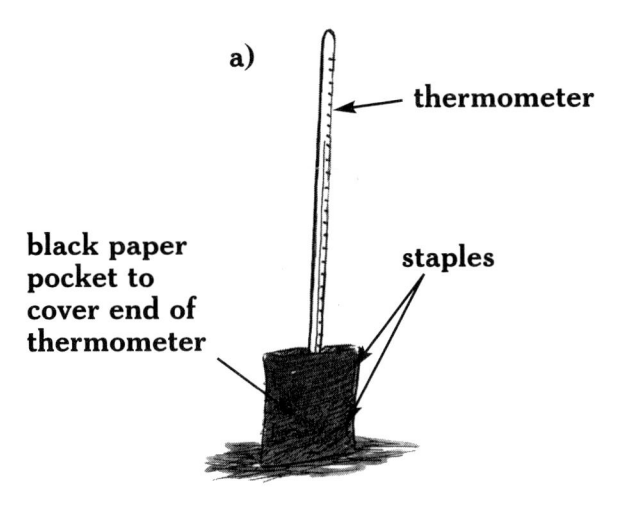

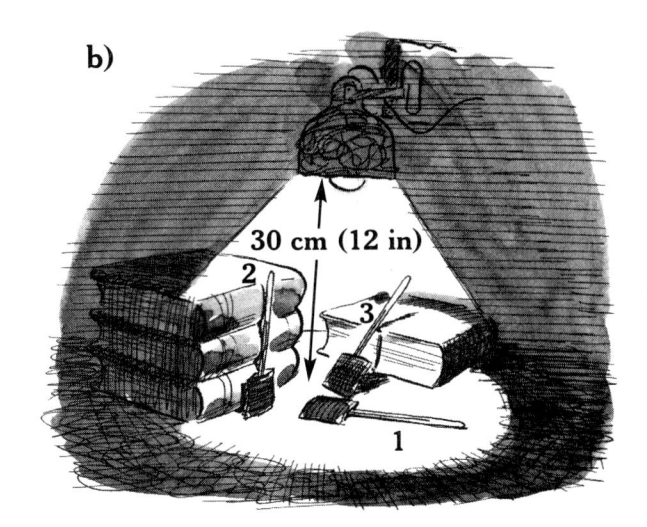

Figure 19.

a) Cut three rectangles from a sheet of black construction paper. Staple them to make pockets to cover the lower (bulb) ends of three identical thermometers. b) Place the three thermometers as shown: 1) flat, at 90 degrees to the light; 2) parallel to the light; 3) at an angle to the light.

construction paper. The pocket is to cover the lower part of the thermometer, as shown in Figure 19a. The size of the cover will depend on the kind of thermometer you use. However, the black paper should completely cover the thermometer bulb and the lower part of the thermometer. It can be stapled as shown.

The three thermometers should be placed at equal distances from a heat lamp, as shown in Figure 19b. One thermometer should lie flat so that the cover is at 90 degrees to the light. A second should be perpendicular to the light; third should be at an angle of about 45 degrees to the light. Use books to prop them up. The light should be centered over the thermometers at a height of about 30 cm (12 in).

All three thermometers should read approximately the same temperature when you turn on the light. Watch the temperature on the flat thermometer. Turn off the lamp after 15 minutes or before the thermometer reaches the end of its temperature range. Read and record the three temperatures.

Which thermometer showed the greatest increase in temperature? Which thermometer showed the least increase in temperature? Do your results confirm what you observed in the previous experiment?

Humidity, Sunshine, and Weather

Experiment 3.6

The Sun's Effect on Earth's Air

Materials

- ✓ **an adult**
- ✓ stove
- ✓ matches
- ✓ upright freezer, such as the freezer compartment above many refrigerators

As you saw in the previous two experiments, the sun provides more heat per area to regions on which it shines more directly. As a result, regions close to the equator receive more energy than do regions farther north or south. To see how the temperature of air affects its movement, you can use a stove, an upright freezer, some matches, and **an adult** to help you.

Turn on a kitchen stove's heating element. This will warm the air above the heating element. **Ask an adult** to light a match. After the match has burned for a few seconds, ask the adult to blow it out and hold it over the heating element. Watch the smoke leaving the match. Which way does it travel? Why do you think it moves that way?

Ask the adult to light another match. While the match is burning, open the door of a freezer at the top of a refrigerator. After the match is extinguished, hold it just below the open freezer door. Which way does the smoke travel this time? Can you explain why it moves as it does?

Experiment 3.7

Hot Air, Cold Air, and Volume

Materials

- ✓ balloon
- ✓ empty 2- or 3-liter soda bottle
- ✓ pail
- ✓ sink
- ✓ hot tap water
- ✓ refrigerator
- ✓ freezer

As you saw in the previous experiment, hot air rises and cold air sinks. But why does air rise when warm and sink when cool?

To find out, pull the neck of a balloon over the mouth of an empty 2- or 3-liter soda bottle. Next, place a pail in a sink and fill it with hot tap water. Put the bottle in the hot water and hold it there. Watch the balloon. What happens to it as the air in the bottle becomes warmer? What happens to air when its temperature rises?

Place the bottle and balloon in a refrigerator. What happens to the balloon as the air in the bottle cools? What happens to air when its temperature decreases?

What do you think will happen if you place the bottle and balloon in a freezer? Try it! What happens? Was your prediction correct?

Humidity, Sunshine, and Weather

Take the bottle out of the freezer and remove the balloon. Fill the bottle with hot tap water. Then empty the bottle. Having filled the bottle with hot water, the air in the bottle will be warm when the water is poured out. Quickly cover the mouth of the bottle with a balloon. Predict what will happen to the balloon as the air in the bottle cools. Did you predict correctly?

Science Project Idea

Design and carry out an experiment to find a mathematical relationship between the volume of a gas and its temperature. You must, of course, keep the pressure constant, because increasing the pressure on a gas will decrease its volume.

AIR'S DENSITY AND TEMPERATURE

As you have seen, air—in fact, any gas—expands when heated and contracts when cooled. Since the weight of the air doesn't change when it is heated, the density of the air must decrease as its temperature rises. Similarly, its density must increase as it cools. (The density of a substance is its weight divided by its volume.) If the volume increases and the weight stays the same, the density must decrease.

Suppose we have one liter of air at a temperature of 20°C (68°F). The air will weigh 1.20 grams. Its density will be:

$$\frac{1.20 \text{ g}}{1.00 \text{ L}} = 1.20 \text{ g/L}$$

If the temperature of the gas rises to 100°C (212°F), its volume will become 1.27 liters. Its density will then be:

$$\frac{1.20 \text{ g}}{1.27 \text{ L}} = 0.945 \text{ g/L}$$

If the temperature of an air mass rises, its volume increases and its density decreases. It will then rise if cooler air is above it. By the same token, if an air mass cools, its volume shrinks and its density increases. It will then sink if there is warmer air beneath it.

As you saw in Experiments 3.4 and 3.5, the sun provides more heat per area to equatorial regions than to places at greater latitude. As a result, air masses tend to rise near the equator. They move north or south as the air is replaced by cooler air flowing toward the equator.

Only 70 percent of the sun's energy that reaches Earth's atmosphere is retained. Thirty percent is reflected back into space. Of the 70 percent that reaches Earth, only 28 percent is absorbed by the atmosphere; the rest is soaked up by water and ground. Some of the solar energy that warms Earth's ground and water flows back into space as infrared radiation, a type of energy that all warm objects release. Radiation of heat into space is particularly evident on clear nights. Temperatures fall quickly after sunset. Less cooling occurs on cloudy nights because the moisture-laden clouds absorb much of the infrared energy and reradiate much of it back to Earth.

On snow-covered ground, 75 to 95 percent of the solar energy is reflected. In addition, the snow itself releases infrared radiation. As a result, polar regions, which receive little solar radiation in the winter to begin with, grow colder with time. During much of its winter, the region releases more energy than it receives.

Experiment 3.8

Transferring Energy to Water and Soil

Materials

- ✓ balance to weigh things
- ✓ 2 Styrofoam cups
- ✓ 2 identical thermometers
- ✓ sand
- ✓ hot and cold water
- ✓ warm sunny place or a heat lamp
- ✓ notebook and pen or pencil
- ✓ clock or watch
- ✓ a cool place

As you have read, much of the sun's energy that reaches Earth is absorbed by land and water. The heat in Earth's surface can be transferred to cooler air in contact with it. How well do different substances absorb radiant energy? In this experiment you will compare the absorption of radiant energy by water and sand.

Place about 150 grams (5 ounces) of sand in a Styrofoam cup. Put a thermometer into the sand. Wait several minutes until the temperature reading stays the same. Place an equal weight of water at the same temperature in a second Styrofoam cup. You can adjust the water temperature by mixing cold and warm water until it matches the temperature of the sand.

With identical thermometers in the two cups, place the cups side by side in a warm sunny place or under a heat lamp. Both sand and water should receive equal amounts of light. Read the temperatures in the two cups at 10-minute intervals. Be careful not to warm either cup beyond the thermometer's maximum temperature. Which substance, water or sand, warms faster given equal quantities of radiant energy? If the temperature of equal weights of sand and water both increased by 20 degrees, which substance would have absorbed more energy?

Given equal weights of water and sand, which substance do you predict will cool faster? To check your prediction, again adjust the water's weight and temperature to match that of the warm sand. Then place both cups side by side in a cool place, such as a refrigerator or basement. Record their temperatures

Humidity, Sunshine, and Weather

at 10-minute intervals. Which substance cools faster? Did you predict it? Which substance held more heat?

You can do this experiment in another way, a way that will ensure that both sand and water receive the same amount of heat.

Prepare the samples of water and sand as before. When they are at the same temperature, remove the thermometer and put the cup with the sand in the center of a microwave oven. Heat the sand for exactly 15 seconds. Remove, stir the sand, and read the final temperature of the sand. Repeat the experiment with the cup of water. What is its final temperature?

Both sand and water received the same amount of heat. Which one showed the greater increase in temperature? Which one would require more heat to raise its temperature by 10°C (18°F)? Which one can hold more heat?

Why do regions near large bodies of water show smaller changes in average seasonal temperatures than those surrounded by land? For example, explain the difference in the graphs of average monthly temperatures for Seattle, Washington, located on the edge of the Pacific Ocean, and Spokane, Washington, located about 300 miles inland (Figure 20).

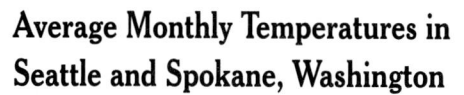

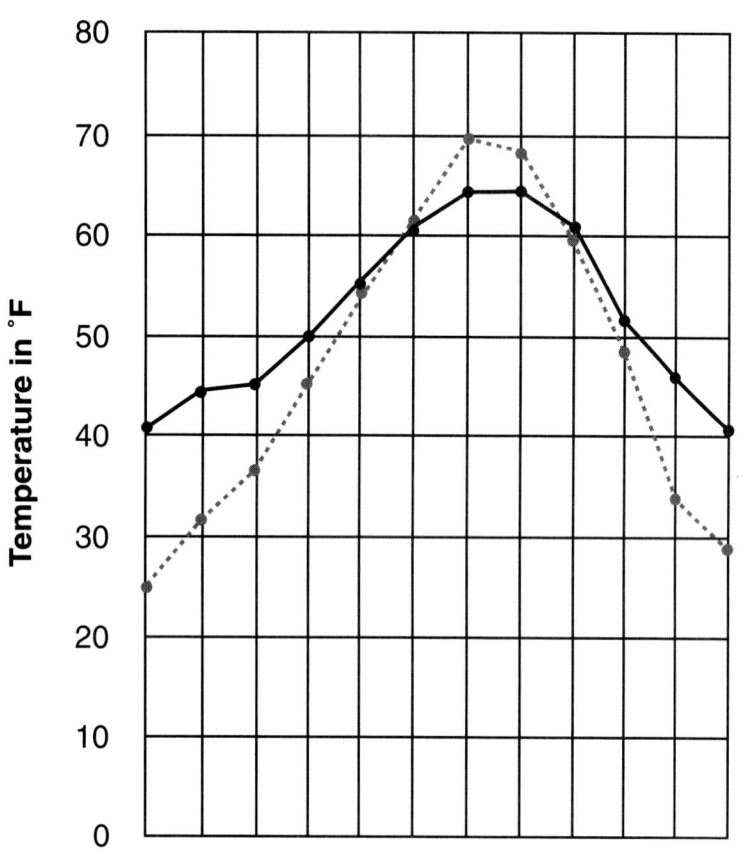

Weather Science Fair Projects

Average Monthly Temperatures in Seattle and Spokane, Washington

Figure 20.

The graph shows the average monthly temperatures in Seattle (on the coast) and Spokane (inland), Washington. The solid line is for Seattle temperatures; the dotted line is for Spokane temperatures.

Humidity, Sunshine, and Weather

Science Project Idea

Expand Experiment 3.8 to include other materials such as gravel, humus, garden soil, rubbing alcohol, cooking oil, and so on. Can any of these substances hold more heat than water or sand?

Experiment 3.9

The Effect of Color on Radiant Energy Absorption

Materials

- ✓ 2 identical thermometers
- ✓ black and white construction paper
- ✓ scissors
- ✓ stapler
- ✓ heat lamp or reflector light and clamp with 75-watt bulb
- ✓ ruler
- ✓ clock or watch
- ✓ notebook and pen or pencil
- ✓ dirt path
- ✓ asphalt path

In Experiment 3.5 you made black pockets to cover the lower parts of the thermometers you used. In this experiment you need to use pieces of black and white construction paper of the same size to make one black and one white cover. Insert identical thermometers into the covers. Place the thermometers in their covers side by side under a source of light energy as you did in Experiment 3.5.

Watch the temperature readings on the thermometers. Turn off the lamp after 15 minutes or before either thermometer reaches the end of its temperature range. Read and record the two temperatures. Which color is a better absorber of light energy?

On a sunny day, place a thermometer on an asphalt path. Place a second thermometer on a dirt path. Which thermometer, if either, do you think will record the higher temperature? Try it! Were you right?

Humidity, Sunshine, and Weather

Science Project Ideas

- Investigate the effect of other colors such as red, orange, yellow, green, blue, and violet on the absorption of light energy. Are any of these colors better absorbers of light than black?

- Design and carry out an experiment to see whether water blackened with ink is a better absorber of light energy than plain, clear water.

- Which liquid, black or clear, will radiate energy faster? Design an experiment to find out.

- Does the color of the clothes you wear outdoors on a sunny day affect the amount of solar energy transferred to your body? Design an experiment to find out.

- Using what you have learned about the absorption of light energy, design a system to heat part of your home with solar energy.

THE WATER CYCLE

Earth's absorption of solar energy moves air, and therefore weather, across land and sea. But this energy also drives the water (hydrologic) cycle, as shown in Figure 21. That is, it provides the energy needed to evaporate water (change liquid water to gaseous water). The gaseous water then condenses as it cools, forming clouds, and falls back to Earth as rain on land as well as water. Water is continually involved in this cycle, evaporating into a gas, condensing into a liquid, and falling back to Earth as rain, only to evaporate again in a never-ending cycle.

In the next experiment you will prepare several models to represent the water cycle.

Figure 21.

The drawing shows the water cycle. The sun provides the heat that evaporates water. The water vapor condenses into water droplets, forming clouds. The droplets combine and fall back to Earth as rain.

Humidity, Sunshine, and Weather

Experiment 3.10

Models of the Hydrologic Cycle

Materials

- ✓ **an adult**
- ✓ teakettle
- ✓ water
- ✓ stove
- ✓ ice cubes
- ✓ clear bowl
- ✓ pot holder
- ✓ hot tap water
- ✓ aluminum pie pan
- ✓ 2 water glasses, one large and one small
- ✓ large plastic box or shoe box lined with plastic wrap
- ✓ stones
- ✓ cold water
- ✓ bright sunshine
- ✓ plastic wrap
- ✓ tape

A BASIC MODEL OF THE WATER CYCLE

The basic principles involved in the water cycle can be demonstrated quite easily. Pour a cup or two of water into a teakettle. Heat the kettle on a stove **under adult supervision.** While the water is heating, add a few ice cubes to a bowl. When you see steam in the air above the kettle spout, **ask an adult** to hold the edge of the bowl with a pot holder. **Have the adult** lift the bowl and hold it above the teakettle's spout. Watch the cold bottom of the bowl. After a short time you should see water vapor condensing into droplets. As the water droplets grow, they eventually fall as "rain."

OTHER MODELS OF THE WATER CYCLE

Half fill a clear bowl with hot tap water. Cover the bowl with an aluminum pie pan. Add ice cubes to the pan. Water will evaporate from the warm water only to condense back to water on the pan. If enough water condenses, the condensed droplets may grow big enough to fall as "rain."

The water in the bowl represents the water in Earth's lakes, rivers, and ocean. What does the cold aluminum pan represent?

An even simpler model can be established with two water glasses, one large and one small. Half fill the smaller glass with hot tap water. Place two ice cubes in the larger glass and place it on top of the smaller glass. Can you see water condensing on the bottom of the large glass? As time passes, can you see it "rain"?

A BETTER MODEL OF THE WATER CYCLE

You can make a better model by using the sun as the source of heat to evaporate water. Find a large plastic box or line a shoe box with plastic wrap. Add stones to one end of the box to represent mountains and soil. Then add water until there is an inch or two of water covering the bottom of the box. Place the box where it will receive warm, bright sunshine. Cover the top of the box with plastic wrap and seal it with tape, as shown in

Humidity, Sunshine, and Weather

Figure 22. Observe the box periodically for several hours. Can you see water droplets forming on the underside of the plastic-wrap cover? Where did that water come from? Do any of those droplets grow and fall as "rain" on the land and sea below? Why is this a better model than the two earlier ones?

Figure 22.

This model of the water cycle uses the sun as the energy source to evaporate the water.

Science Project Idea

Design and make a model of your own to demonstrate the water cycle.

Experiment 3.11

Factors Affecting the Evaporation of Water

Materials

- ✓ paper towels
- ✓ hot and cold water
- ✓ clothespins
- ✓ clothesline
- ✓ bright sunshine
- ✓ cardboard boxes
- ✓ a fan

Soak a paper towel in hot tap water; soak an identical paper towel in cold water. Hang both towels outside on a clothesline in bright sunshine, as shown in Figure 23a. Which towel is the first to dry? How does temperature affect the rate of evaporation?

Soak two identical paper towels in cold water. Fold one towel again and again until it is a small rectangle. Leave the second towel unfolded. Hang both towels on a clothesline in

Humidity, Sunshine, and Weather

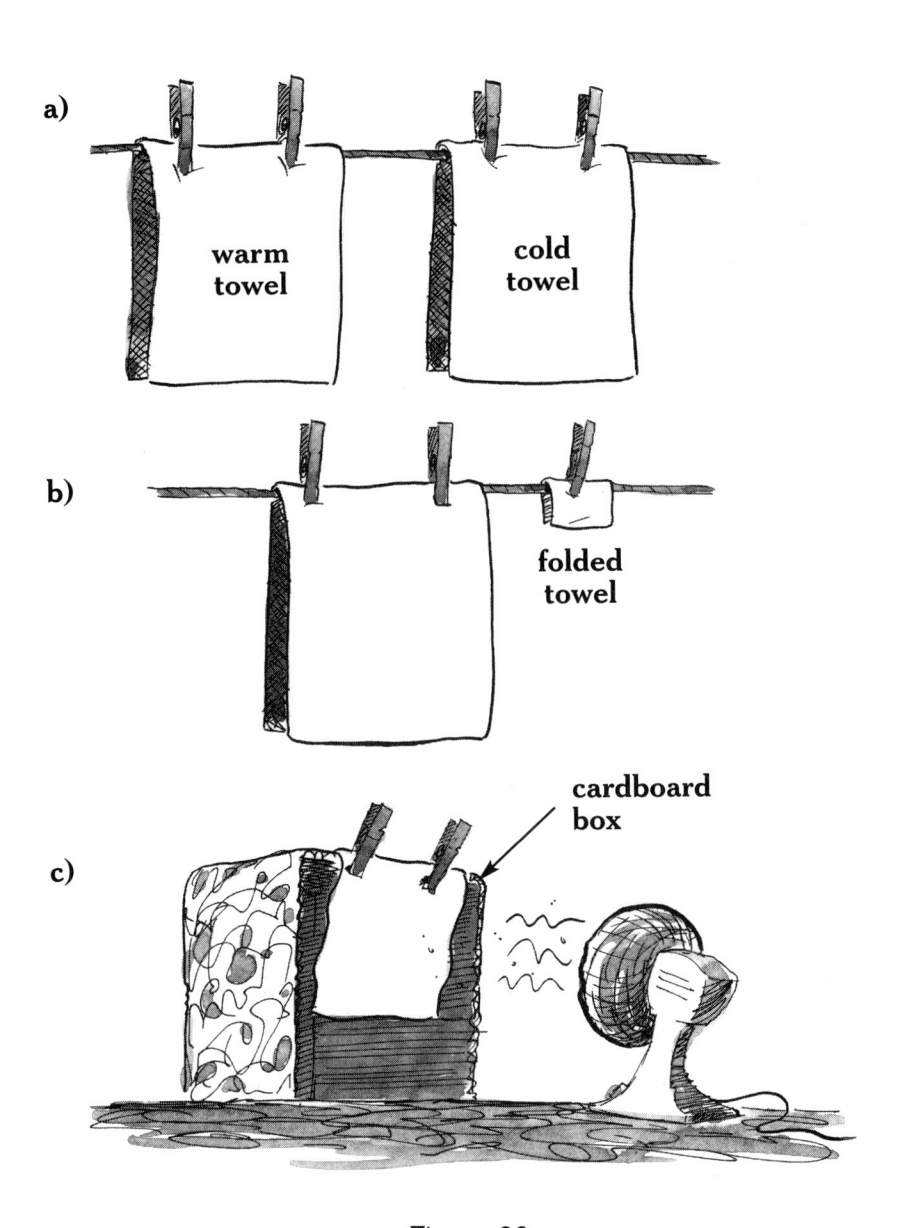

Figure 23.

These experiments show how evaporation is affected by a) temperature; b) surface area; c) moving air.

bright sunshine, as shown in Figure 23b. Which towel dries first? How does surface area exposed to air affect the rate at which water evaporates?

Soak two identical paper towels in tap water. Lay an open cardboard box on its side and hang one towel from its edge. Put the box on one side of a room, garage, or basement. Hang the other towel on a second box. Use a fan to move air across one towel but not the other. (See Figure 23c.) Which towel dries first? How does moving air affect the rate at which water evaporates?

Explain why each of the factors you tested affects the rate of evaporation.

Two lakes hold the same volume of water and are near one another. One lake covers twice as much area as the first. From which lake will more water evaporate each day?

Science Project Idea

Design an experiment that will enable you to measure the rate of evaporation under different conditions.

Chapter 4

Air and Wind Patterns on a Spinning Globe

As you have seen, the sun provides the energy to evaporate water. The gaseous water cools as it ascends into the atmosphere, condenses to form clouds, and eventually falls back to Earth as rain, snow, sleet, or hail. The sun's uneven heating of Earth gives rise to air masses of different temperatures and, therefore, of different densities. The warmer, less dense air rises as it is replaced by cooler air. Ascending or descending air masses are called air currents. Sometimes vertical movement of air is quite noticeable. You may have seen birds gliding upward on an ascending current of air. At other times, the air is quite stable; that is, there are no vertical air currents. Why do you think that might happen?

Experiment 4.1

Stable and Unstable Air

Materials

- ✓ **an adult**
- ✓ hot and cold water
- ✓ ice cubes
- ✓ small glass
- ✓ blue or green food coloring
- ✓ plastic vial
- ✓ long eyedropper
- ✓ thermometer
- ✓ heated room

Weather reports sometimes refer to stable or unstable air. A meteorologist might say, "We have a stable air mass. A layer of warm air is sitting above cold air." Or she might say, "The air is unstable today because the warm air you feel is covered by cold air aloft."

To see how the temperatures of cold and warm layers of air affect atmospheric stability, you can do an experiment using water. Both water and air are fluids because both can flow. As a result, they behave similarly under many conditions. First, prepare some cold water by adding several ice cubes to a small glass of water. Add a few drops of blue or green food coloring to the cold water and stir. Next, nearly fill a plastic vial or small

Air and Wind Patterns on a Spinning Globe

glass with hot tap water. Use a long eyedropper to remove some of the cold colored water from the glass. Place the tip of the eyedropper on the bottom of the vial of hot water, as shown in Figure 24. Very gently squeeze the eyedropper bulb to place a layer of cold water below the hot water. Keep the bulb compressed as you slowly lift the eyedropper from the vial. Leave the vial where it will be undisturbed while you do the second part of the experiment.

Again, prepare some cold water as you did before, but do not add food coloring. Instead, add the food coloring to a glass of hot tap water and stir. Now fill a vial or small glass with the cold water. Use the eyedropper to remove some of the hot colored water from the glass. Place the tip of the eyedropper on the bottom of the vial of cold water and gently squeeze the eyedropper bulb. Keep the bulb compressed as you slowly lift the eyedropper from the vial. Can you see a layer of hot water beneath the cold water? Or does the warm water rise to the top of the cold water? Compare the two vials. In which vial were the layers more stable?

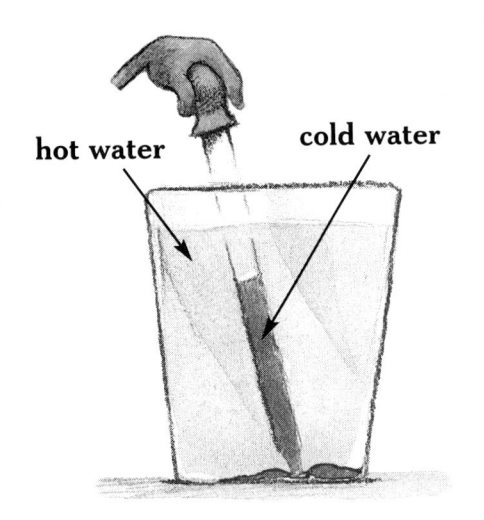

Figure 24.

Carefully place a layer of cold colored water under some warm water. Are the layers stable?

93

Why is a layer of warm air over a layer of cold air more stable than the reverse?

As you probably know, objects more dense than water sink in water, while objects less dense than water float. A block of wood floats on water. Wood is less dense than water. A steel washer sinks in water. Steel is more dense than water. Your experiment shows that warm water is less dense than cold water.

To see that air behaves in a similar way, place a thermometer near the floor of a room. After several minutes, record the temperature. Then **ask an adult to hold** the thermometer near the ceiling for several minutes. Why is the air near the ceiling warmer than the air near the floor?

In the next experiment you will investigate what causes air to move horizontally; that is, what causes winds to blow.

Experiment 4.2

What Causes Winds?

Materials

✓ balloon
✓ bicycle tire pump

Wind is the movement of air over Earth's surface. For anything to move, a force must act on it. To discover the force causing air to move, fill a balloon with air. Squeeze the neck of the balloon so that the air inside cannot escape. With your other hand, push inward on the balloon's surface. Do you feel an opposing

Air and Wind Patterns on a Spinning Globe

force? Do you feel a force that is as strong when you push against air outside the balloon? Do you think the pressure is greater inside or outside the balloon? What makes you think so?

Hold the mouth of the balloon near your face. Then slightly release your grip on the balloon's neck. Can you feel a wind moving against your face? Why do you think air is flowing out of the balloon?

You can use a bicycle tire pump to see a similar effect. To increase the pressure in a tire, you use a pump to force air into the tire. Because air is squeezed into the tire, there are more air molecules per cubic centimeter inside the tire than there are outside. Another way of saying this is that the air pressure is greater inside than outside the tire. A tire pump, as shown in Figure 25, squeezes air together. Pushing more air into a confined space increases the pressure. Place the end of

Figure 25.
When the pump's piston is pushed into the cylinder, the valve closes and air in the cylinder is forced into a smaller volume. When the piston moves back, the valve opens and air enters the cylinder.

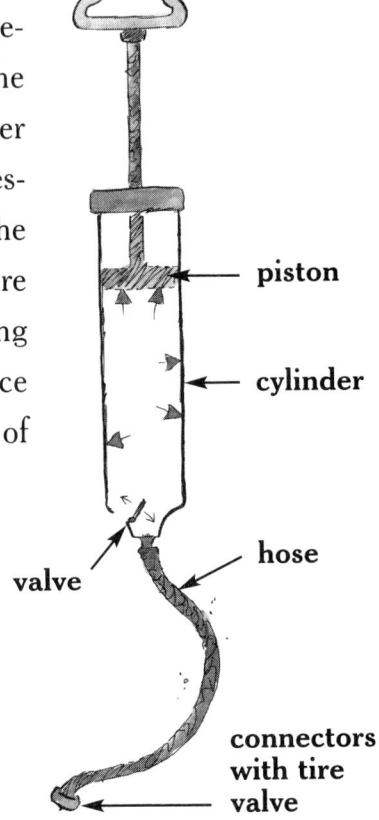

the pump's hose near your face as you push the piston down. Can you feel a wind blowing onto your skin? What do you think causes the wind?

Experiment 4.3

Winds: A Complication

Materials

- ✓ ball
- ✓ level floor or walk
- ✓ cardboard
- ✓ turntable or lazy Susan
- ✓ felt-tip pen
- ✓ ruler
- ✓ a partner

As you learned in the previous experiment, winds are caused by air moving from high pressure to low pressure. If we lived on a frictionless Earth that did not rotate, pressure differences alone could account for wind speed and direction. However, we live on a planet that turns and one on which friction is common.

Give a ball a push to start it rolling along a level floor or walk. You will see the ball slow down and eventually stop. Friction between the ball and the surface it rolls over acts against the ball's motion, causing it to eventually stop. When air moves over Earth, it rubs against trees, grass, water, buildings, and so on. The air's velocity, like that of a rolling ball, is reduced by friction.

Air and Wind Patterns on a Spinning Globe

But there is another more subtle factor that can change the direction of a moving air mass. It is known as the Coriolis effect, caused by Earth's rotation.

If you were to stand still at the North Pole, the ground you stood on would simply rotate in place. You would not move from your spot and would, therefore, have no velocity. At the equator, however, you would be traveling from west to east at a great speed. Since the equator is 40,086 km (24,900 miles) around and the Earth turns once every 24 hours, anything resting on the equator moves at a speed of 1,670 km/hr (1,038 mi/hr), because:

$$\frac{40,086 \text{ km}}{24 \text{ hr}} = 1,670 \text{ km/hr}$$

To visualize the Coriolis effect, cut a piece of cardboard to match the circular top of a turntable, a piano stool that can spin, or a lazy Susan. Think of the center of the cardboard as the Earth's North Pole. The circumference of the cardboard can be considered to be Earth's equator. How far will a point at the center of the rotating circle (North Pole) move in one revolution? How fast will it move? How about the outer edge of the cardboard (the region similar to Earth's equator)—how far does it move in one revolution? What will be its speed if it turns once every second?

Next, consider a point halfway between the center and the rim of the circle (an Earth latitude of 45 degrees). How far

97

does it move in one revolution? What will be its speed if it rotates once every second? Which points on the circle move fastest? Slowest?

Suppose the circle is rotating counterclockwise, like the Earth does as seen from above the North Pole. If you were to try to draw a straight line outward from the center of the circle (North Pole) to the edge (equator), what do you think it would look like?

With a felt-tip pen, lightly draw a straight line (a radius) from the center of the cardboard to its edge. Next, repeat the process while the cardboard is turning. How does this line compare with the previous one? Can you explain why they differ?

If you doubt that you really drew a straight line, hold a ruler beside the pen just above the cardboard circle to guide the pen as you draw the line. Notice how the easterly rotation of the cardboard, as seen from the "North Pole," causes the line to curve to the right (west).

Here is a way to better understand what caused the curved line when the disk was turning. Have someone slowly turn the lazy Susan, piano seat, or turntable counterclockwise as you slowly move the pen straight out from the center of the cardboard circle.

Repeat the experiment, but this time draw a straight line from the edge (equator) of the circle to the center (North Pole). Again, you'll see that the line is curved and seems to bend. Does it bend toward the right or the left?

Air and Wind Patterns on a Spinning Globe

Why do the straight lines that you drew appear as curved lines on the rotating cardboard?

Look closely at the lines you drew on the rotating circle. Where are the lines blurred the most? Why?

Winds moving across Earth's Northern Hemisphere appear to shift to the right, just as the pen did when you pulled it in a straight line across the rotating disk. Suppose a cold mass of air begins moving southward from the North Pole into a warmer, less dense air mass to the south. Its eastward velocity at the pole is zero. But as it moves south, the Earth's eastward speed increases (see Figure 26). Since the air moving south has no eastward velocity, it seems to be moving westward (to the right of its path) to people on Earth because they are moving more rapidly eastward than the southbound air (see Figure 27).

You see or feel a similar effect when you ride your bike on a calm day. It feels as if a wind is blowing at you because you are moving through still air. On the other hand, if you ride southward at 10 mph when there is a 10 mph north wind (blowing north to south), you feel no wind. From your point of view, the wind speed is zero.

For similar reasons, south winds (blowing northward) in our hemisphere appear to be shifted eastward (to the right) because they start with a larger eastward velocity than do points on Earth north of the moving air mass.

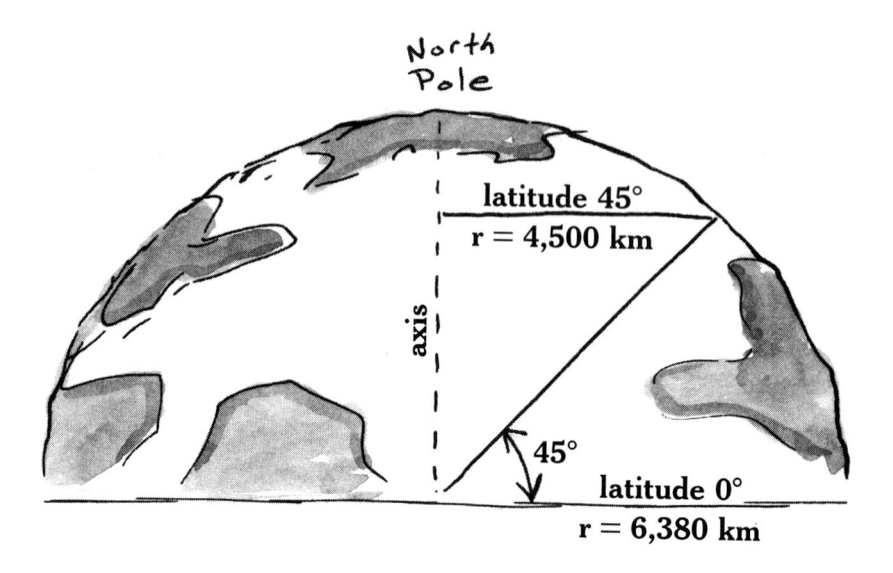

```
                    North
                    Pole
                        |
                        |-----latitude 45°
                        |     r = 4,500 km
                        |
                   axis |
                        |
                        |
                        |     45°
                        |     ↓  latitude 0°
                              r = 6,380 km
```

Figure 26.

At the equator, the distance from Earth's axis (the line about which it turns) is 6,380 kilometers (3,960 miles). At 45 degrees latitude, as the drawing shows, the distance from Earth's axis to its surface is only 4,500 kilometers (2,800 miles). Points on Earth's equator move eastward at a speed of 1,670 kilometers per hour (1,038 miles per hour). At a latitude of 45 degrees, points on Earth's surface move eastward at 1,180 kilometers per hour (730 miles per hour), or about seven-tenths as fast as points on the equator. At what speeds do points at 30 and 60 degrees latitude move about Earth's axis?

Water currents in the ocean, such as the Gulf Stream that flows northward from the Gulf of Mexico, are also bent due to Earth's rotation. The shift of winds and ocean currents to the right of their path in the Northern Hemisphere (to the left in the Southern Hemisphere) is caused by Earth's rotation.

Air and Wind Patterns on a Spinning Globe

You may have heard that the Coriolis effect causes water to always turn clockwise as it enters a drain in the Northern Hemisphere and that is turns counterclockwise in drains south of the equator. Look closely at water entering drains in your sinks, showers, and bathtubs for several weeks. Does the water always curl clockwise as it drains?

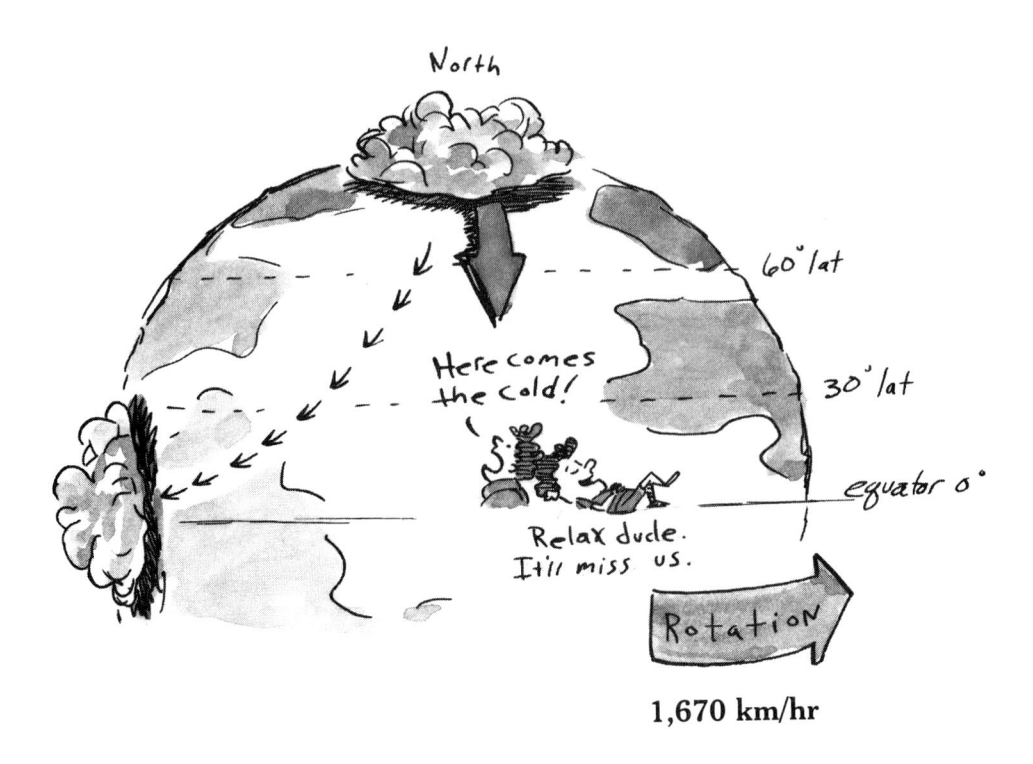

Figure 27.
Air masses moving southward in the Northern Hemisphere appear to turn westward because of Earth's eastward rotation. At the equator, all points on Earth's surface move eastward at 1,670 kilometers per hour (1,038 miles per hour).

Science Project Ideas

- While the cardboard disk is turning, can you move the pen so as to draw a line from the center to the edge that really is straight? Can you draw a straight line on the rotating circle when you move the pen from the edge to the center?

- What is the eastward velocity of points at 30 and 60 degrees latitude?

- What would be the apparent path of air masses moving northward in the Southern Hemisphere? Of air masses moving south in the Southern Hemisphere?

- Take a ride on a merry-go-round. Where should you sit or stand to get the fastest ride? Where should you sit or stand to get the slowest ride?

- Why are people not allowed to walk on a merry-go-round while it is moving?

Air and Wind Patterns on a Spinning Globe

JET STREAMS

Jet streams, as defined by the World Meteorological Organization, are winds with speeds equal to or greater than 58 knots (108 kph, or 67 mph) that are thousands of miles long, hundreds of miles wide, and a few thousand feet deep. They are found at the troposphere and were discovered by pilots during World War II. To reach altitudes exceeding the range of antiaircraft guns, these pilots flew at altitudes of 30,000 feet or more. The pilots found that relative to the ground, their planes sometimes were barely moving or moving faster than ever before. They realized they were experiencing headwinds or tailwinds with velocities as great as 400 kph (250 mph).

After the war, meteorologists investigated these winds. They found the winds (jet streams) generally moved from west to east along wavelike paths that carried them north and south of their overall direction. Today, planes flying east will often take advantage of jet-stream tailwinds to save fuel. Westward bound planes try to avoid jet-stream headwinds.

Jet streams form where warm air masses moving north from equatorial regions meet cold air flowing south. If the northward-moving air begins near the equator, it has a large eastward velocity due to Earth's rotation. As it moves northward, Earth beneath it is moving more slowly.

The warm northward-moving air with its eastward velocity due to the Coriolis effect collides with colder air, giving rise to a jet stream. The stream, in general, follows the boundary between warm and cold air and gives rise to high- and low-pressure cells. Regions south of the jet stream are generally warmer than regions north of that stream. Watch for diagrams of the jet stream in your region on TV weather reports. You will see that local temperatures are strongly influenced by your position relative to the jet stream.

There are several jet streams moving about Earth in both hemispheres at different latitudes. Average jet-stream wind velocities in the winter are about 160 kph (100 mph); summer jet streams average about half that speed.

Chapter 5

Clouds and Stormy Weather

We all enjoy the beauty of a bright blue sky and clear dry air. However, we need water to drink and to nourish the green plants that provide us with food and oxygen. Water falls to Earth from moisture-laden clouds. The clouds reflect much of the sun's energy back into space, which keeps Earth's temperatures at moderate levels. Clouds also reflect some of the energy emitted by Earth back to its surface. That is why temperatures drop less dramatically on cloudy nights. On clear nights, radiant energy from Earth can flow into outer space. In this chapter you will investigate the formation of clouds and storms. All storms are characterized by clouds, but some are dangerous because they also contain damaging winds, and dangerous electrical energy, and sometimes severe flooding.

Experiment 5.1

Recipe for a Cloud

Materials

- ✓ thermometer
- ✓ spray can (air freshener can is good)
- ✓ air pump
- ✓ metal jar lid
- ✓ clear plastic container that can be sealed
- ✓ table salt (sodium chloride)
- ✓ warm water

In Chapter 3 you saw how water evaporates and falls back to Earth as rain. You learned, too, that water vapor must cool in order to condense and form clouds. As moist air rises, its pressure decreases. There is less air above pushing on it. When air, or any gas, expands, it cools. You can do a simple experiment to see that this is true.

Place a thermometer about a foot from the nozzle of a spray can. One that sprays an air freshener works well. The vapor within the can is under pressure. It will expand when released. Note the temperature on the thermometer. Then press the nozzle button so that the expanding vapor strikes the thermometer bulb. What happens to the temperature? Why?

Clouds and Stormy Weather

You can do another experiment to show that compressing a gas (squeezing its molecules closer together) produces heat. Use an air pump to increase the pressure in a bicycle tire. (If necessary, you can first release some air from the tire.) After you have pumped for a while, feel the connection between the pump's cylinder and the tube that leads to the tire. What has happened to its temperature? How can you explain its change in temperature?

Moisture and cooling by expansion are not the only ingredients needed for cloud formation. The water vapor needs tiny particles, nuclei, on which to condense. Without these nuclei, water vapor can cool to temperatures as low as $-40°C$ ($-40°F$) without condensing.

Normally, these nuclei are tiny salt crystals carried into the air by updrafts when ocean waves break as they strike shore. The crystals are only about a tenth of a micron in diameter (0.00001 cm). But you can use crystals of a visible size to see what happens in a cloud.

Find a metal jar lid. You also need a clear plastic container that can be sealed. Sprinkle a few crystals of table salt (sodium chloride) on the top of the jar lid. Place the jar lid on the bottom of the container. Pour enough warm water into the container (but not in the lid) to cover its bottom. Then put the top on the container to seal it. The water will evaporate, filling the container with water vapor.

After about 15 minutes, open the container and look at the salt crystals. Notice that they have been replaced by tiny hemispheres of water. The salt particles served as nuclei on which the vapor condensed.

If the air is dry, you can remove the metal lid and watch the salt crystals re-form, as the water in which they are dissolved evaporates.

Science Project Idea

Design and carry out an experiment to detect the tiny particles found in air. Then develop a way to find the number of particles per cubic yard or meter.

Experiment 5.2

Making a Cloud

Materials

- ✓ **an adult**
- ✓ clear, empty, 2-liter plastic soda bottle and cap
- ✓ warm water
- ✓ matches

A cloud is a huge mass of water droplets. As you have seen, warm air expands as it rises and cools. Because cold air

Clouds and Stormy Weather

cannot hold as much water vapor as warm air, some of the water vapor may condense on very small particles to form water droplets.

Most of the particles on which the vapor condenses come from the ocean. Breaking waves create bubbles that burst, sending tiny particles of salt into the atmosphere. The droplets that form around the salt particles are too light to fall in the strong air currents. But as the small drops bump into one another, they combine into larger drops and may eventually fall to the ground as raindrops. Each raindrop may be made from as many as a million tiny cloud droplets.

If the air in a cloud is very cold, the drops can freeze into small ice crystals, which grow bigger through collisions with smaller droplets. Falling through the bottom of the cloud, the ice crystals may melt into raindrops or fall as snowflakes. Whether they fall as rain or snow depends on the air temperature.

You may have accidentally made a cloud when you opened a can or bottle of cold soda on a hot day. The cloud probably appeared briefly just above the opening. When you opened the can, the gas pressure inside was released. The sudden drop in pressure allowed vapor to expand, cool, and condense.

You can make a cloud quite easily. Remove any labels from a clear, empty, 2-liter plastic soda bottle. Pour about half a cup of warm water into the bottle. Screw on the cap and shake the bottle to saturate the air inside with water vapor. Hold the bottle up against a light background such as a window. Shake the bottle again. Then squeeze and release it. You will probably not see a cloud because one ingredient is missing—condensation nuclei.

Ask an adult to light a match, blow it out, and quickly lower the match into the mouth of the bottle so that smoke particles can form inside the bottle. Put the cap back on and again shake the bottle, hold it up against a light background, and squeeze it to increase the pressure inside the bottle. Then suddenly release your squeeze. This will decrease the pressure inside the bottle, allowing the water vapor to expand and cool. You should see a cloud form.

Science Project Ideas

- Find a place in an open field or on the top of a hill where you can see a lot of the sky. Lie down and watch the clouds. Look for clouds that have special shapes.

    Watch the same cloud for a long time. Does it change shape more on the top or on the bottom? See if you can spot a cloud that slowly gets bigger or one that gets smaller. Try to figure out why these changes occur.

Clouds and Stormy Weather

* Design and carry out an experiment to measure the size of raindrops. Does the size change as a storm progresses?

* You can capture and preserve snowflakes. You can then examine them under a microscope. Place some microscope slides on a thin sheet of wood, such as a shingle. Put the slides in a cold, protected place that is below 32°F (0°C). Put a spray can of clear Krylon lacquer in the same cold place. Once the slides and lacquer are cold, spray a thin coat of lacquer on each slide. Hold the wood sheet with the slides in the falling snow until a few flakes collect on each slide. Put the slides back in the same cold place overnight so that the lacquer can dry. Bring the slides inside and examine them under a microscope. What additional experiments can you do using this technique?

KINDS OF CLOUDS

If you have watched clouds carefully, you know they vary greatly in appearance. Meteorologists classify clouds into three main types: cirrus, cumulus, and stratus.

Cirrus clouds are thin, curly, and wispy. When blown into feathery strands, cirrus clouds are called mares' tails.

Cumulus clouds are the puffy, lumpy, fair-weather clouds commonly seen on warm summer afternoons. The tops of cumulus clouds reflect the brilliant white sunlight, but their bases are darker because they are shaded by the cloud above.

Stratus clouds are layered, or stratified, and may blanket the entire sky, bringing rain or snow.

To classify clouds according to their location in the atmosphere, meteorologists use three prefixes. The prefix *cirro-* indicates that the clouds are high, at 6,100 meters (20,000 ft) or more. *Alto-* is used for clouds of middle altitude, about 2,000 to 6,100 meters (6,500 to 20,000 ft). *Strato-* means low-altitude clouds, from ground level (as in fog) to 2,000 meters (6,500 ft). Another prefix, *nimbo-*, or the suffix *-nimbus*, is used to indicate rain-laden clouds.

Using these names, you can arrive at the ten basic types of clouds shown in Table 4.

Table 4.
THE TEN TYPES OF CLOUDS, THEIR APPEARANCE, AND THE APPROXIMATE HEIGHTS AT WHICH THEY ARE FOUND.

Type	Appearance	Height, meters	Height, feet
cirrus	thin, wispy, feathery	6,100 +	20,000 +
cirrostratus	layered, rain-producing	6,100 +	20,000 +
cirrocumulus	puffy, lumpy, fair weather	6,100 +	20,000 +
altostratus	layered, rain-producing	2,000–6,100	6,500–20,000
altocumulus	puffy, lumpy, fair weather	2,000–6,100	6,500–20,000
stratus	layered, rain-producing	0–2,000	0–6,500
nimbostratus	layered, rain-producing	0–2,000	0–6,500
stratocumulus	puffy, lumpy, fair weather	0–2,000	0–6,500
cumulus	puffy, lumpy, fair weather	low–2,000	low–6,500
cumulonimbus	puffy, lumpy, rain-producing	low–12,000	low–40,000

From your own weather records, you know that clouds can help you predict the weather. Often, a weather change is indicated by a change in clouds.

If conditions are right, a cumulus cloud can grow into a towering thunderhead called a cumulonimbus. Violent updrafts of wind may lift the top of the storm cloud to the tropopause.

Cirrus clouds often signal the approach of rain. Dark stratus clouds form when the air is laden with water droplets. They usually accompany rain or snow.

THUNDERSTORMS

Thunderstorms are common on warm, humid summer days. The warm, moisture-laden air rises, often pushed upward by an approaching cold front. As it expands and cools, the water vapor condenses into a cumulus cloud. The heat produced by condensation warms the air, adding fuel to the updraft, which causes the cloud to grow taller. Often the cloud takes the shape of an anvil (an upside-down triangle) as it reaches the tropopause.

As the cumulonimbus cloud grows, strong updrafts keep raindrops from falling. But when temperatures within the upper cloud fall to the freezing point, the water droplets grow larger. Eventually the rising air currents can no longer overcome the gravitational forces on the large drops and they begin to fall. The precipitation produces downdrafts that

Clouds and Stormy Weather

eliminate the humid updrafts, thereby cutting off the needed "fuel" supply. The storm destroys itself.

As you know, thunderstorms are accompanied by lightning and booming noises. For reasons not well understood, the top of a cumulonimbus cloud becomes positively charged, while the lower part becomes negatively charged. When the electrical potential energy reaches a critical level, charges flow across the cloud, creating lightning. The first lightning strikes are within the cloud. Lightning from cloud to ground starts with a thin leader that is followed by a much stronger return stroke from ground to cloud. A single lightning bolt oscillates back and forth many times in less than a second. Charges on Earth are attracted to opposite charges at the base of a cloud. Consequently, tall objects are more likely to be struck by lightning because they are closer to the charged clouds. There is no limit to the number of times they can be struck.

Thunder is heard shortly after the lightning because the air around the lightning bolt is heated to temperatures as high as 54,000°F (30,000°C). The heated air expands suddenly, creating a sound wave. On a much smaller scale, it is expanding air that makes the pop when a balloon breaks.

HURRICANES

Hurricanes are gigantic storms that form over tropical oceans where water temperatures are 27°C (80°F) or higher. Their winds often exceed 240 kph (150 mph) and cover an area 640 km (400 mi) in diameter.

Most of the hurricanes that affect the United States begin as a mass of thunderstorms in the Atlantic Ocean near the bulging west coast of Africa. If the winds increase to 118 kph (74 mph), it is classified as a hurricane. For a hurricane to form, converging winds near the surface are needed to push the warm, moist air upward. Further, winds around the storm need to move at about the same speed at all altitudes so that the storm is not torn apart. In the Northern Hemisphere, as the surface winds converge, the Coriolis effect causes the air to turn in a counterclockwise motion.

Energy to fuel the storm comes from the heat released as large amounts of ascending water condense. The heat warms the air, carrying it farther upward. Air near the surface moves in to replace the rising air, creating the high winds that define a hurricane. Characteristically, a hurricane has an eye about 19 to 40 km (12 to 25 mi) across. The eye is a high-pressure region where warm air is descending, winds are light, and skies are often fair. See the vertical section of a hurricane shown in Figure 28a and the satellite view in Figure 28b.

Atlantic Ocean hurricanes often strike the islands of the West Indies in the Caribbean and continue into the Gulf of Mexico. But sometimes a hurricane will turn northward and move up the East Coast as far as Maine. Once a hurricane moves inland, it lacks the moisture needed to fuel it and begins

Clouds and Stormy Weather

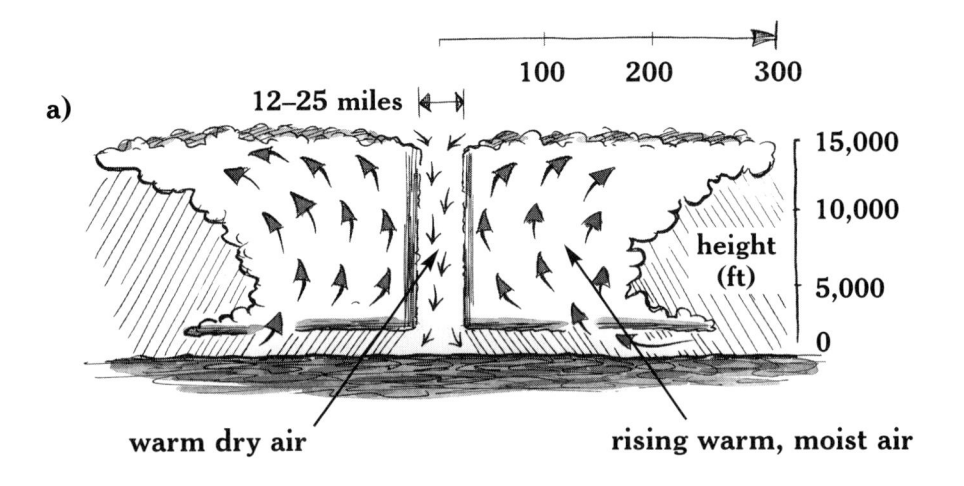

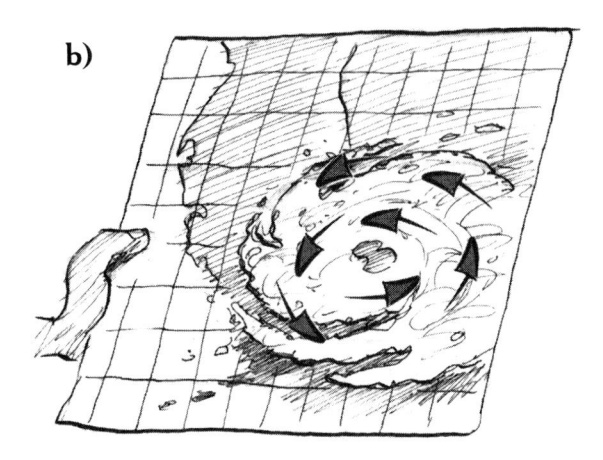

Figure 28.
a) A vertical section of a hurricane. Note the warm, dry air that descends in the eye of the storm. b) A satellite view of the hurricane shows air moving counterclockwise about the eye of the storm.

to dissipate. However, as it approaches land, the storm's low pressure and winds create a mound of water that can inflict serious damage to coastal areas.

Experiment 5.3

Thunder and Lightning

Materials

✓ wire ✓ 6-volt dry cell

You can produce a miniature lightning strike quite easily. Like the top and bottom of a cloud, the two poles of a battery can accumulate opposite (positive and negative) charges. Of course, the battery cannot separate as much charge as a cloud, but you should be able to generate a small spark of "lightning." To produce a mini-stroke of lightning, attach one end of a wire to the positive or negative pole of a 6-volt dry cell. Then touch the other end of the wire to the other pole of the battery. Can you see a small stroke of "lightning"?

The lightning you make with a battery may produce a small sound, but nothing like the thunder that follows natural lightning. Since light travels at 186,000 miles per second, you see lightning almost the instant it occurs. But sound travels much more slowly, about 340 m (1,100 feet) per second, which is about one mile in five seconds. If you see lightning, start counting: "One thousand one, one thousand two, one thousand

Clouds and Stormy Weather

three, . . ." until you hear the thunder. How can you use this technique to estimate the distance to a thunderstorm?

Do not go outside even if a thunderstorm seems far away. Estimate the distance to the storm from inside your house, where it is safer.

TORNADOES

Tornadoes are rapidly rotating winds that blow around a small area of extreme low pressure. A thin funnel cloud may extend to the ground. It rotates in a counterclockwise direction when viewed from above. The funnel cloud usually picks up dust and debris, which makes its tip appear dark and ominous.

Tornadoes are spawned by severe thunderstorms in unstable air where a wedge of cold, dry air flows above a mass of warm, humid air. As the jet stream carries away the cold air, warm air from below is drawn up to replace it.

The first sign of a tornado are rotating clouds that bulge from the base of a thunderstorm. If the rotating clouds continue to move down, a thin funnel may form within the cloud wall and extend toward the ground. The destructive tip of the funnel may bob up and down, skipping some places and causing devastation in others.

Tornadoes are the most powerful kind of storm, but they are usually small in diameter. A funnel tube is usually only 90–545m (100 to 600 yd) wide. Most tornadoes move slowly, at a speed of about 32–64 kph (20 to 40 mph), and last for only a few minutes. The whirling winds near the center, or vortex, of the funnel often exceed 480 kph (300 mph).

Experiment 5.4

A Liquid Tornado

Materials

- ✓ two 2-liter plastic soda bottles
- ✓ water
- ✓ masking or duct tape
- ✓ food coloring

You can make a liquid tornado with two plastic soda bottles, colored water, and tape. Fill one bottle about three-fourths full with water and add a few drops of food coloring. Tape the mouths of the bottles together with masking or duct tape, as shown in Figure 29.

To make the tornado, turn over the joined bottles so that the one with water is on top. Immediately swirl the bottles around rapidly for about 5 seconds, then place them on a table. As the water drains into the lower bottle, a whirling tornado-like funnel should form. Does your liquid tornado twist clockwise or counterclockwise? How can you make one that turns in the other direction?

Clouds and Stormy Weather

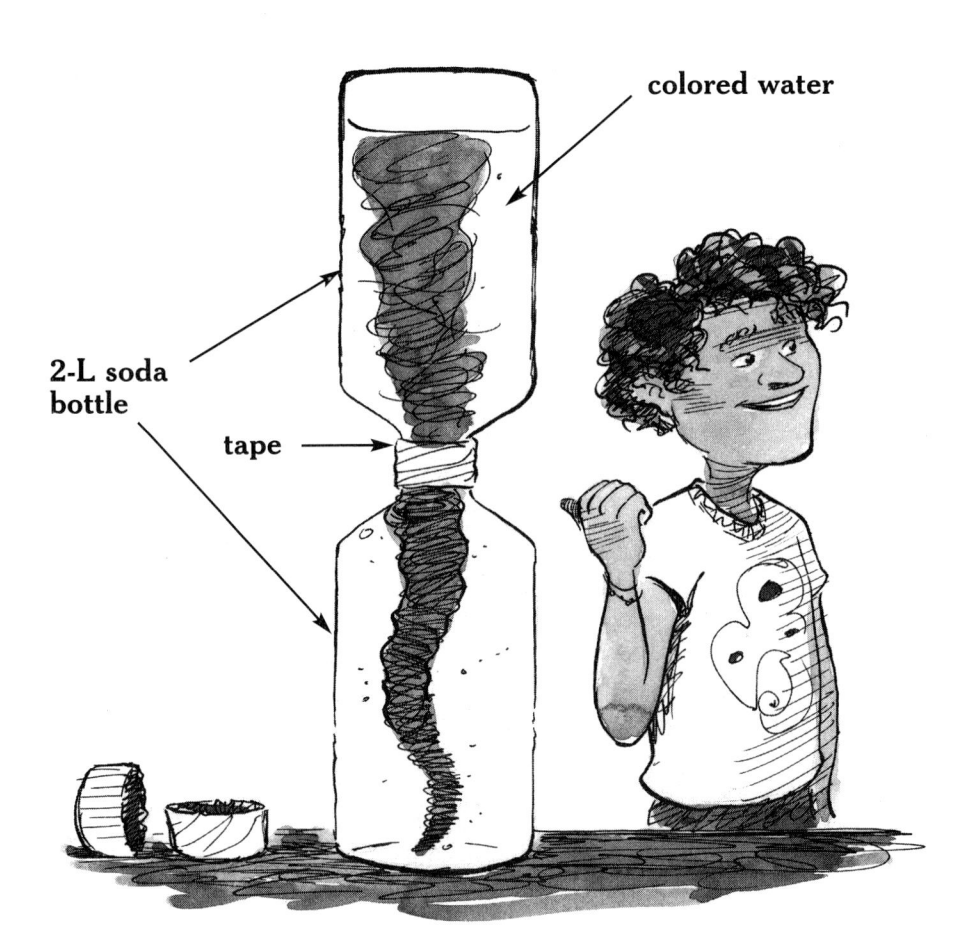

Figure 29.
You can make a liquid tornado.

Chapter 6

Forecasting Weather

By now, your daily weather records, together with what you have learned by doing the experiments in this book, should enable you to begin to make local weather forecasts. Don't worry about making mistakes—even the forecasts of professional meteorologists are correct only about 70 percent of the time. With experience, your forecasts will become more accurate.

As you have learned, useful data for local weather forecasting come from barometer and thermometer readings, wind directions, and cloud types. What type of weather often accompanies increasing air pressure? What weather follows rapidly

Forecasting Weather

falling air pressure? How can you use cloud types to predict the weather? For example, what would you predict if you saw cumulonimbus clouds forming? What would cloudy night skies suggest about the possibility of dew or frost? How about clear night skies? How are shifts in wind direction useful in predicting the weather?

Meteorologists who forecast the weather have a great advantage over you. They base their forecasts on information from a wide variety of sources, extending from satellites far above Earth to instrument-bearing buoys located way out in the ocean, to local weather stations spread across the world that gather data similar to the data you collect in your own station. All this data is transferred to computers programmed to process the information. In addition, forecasters have access to severe weather centers that keep watch for tornadoes, hurricanes, and severe thundershowers.

Once you've developed your forecasting skills, you may want to learn more about weather and its causes. To do that, you need to study science and mathematics. Meteorology is very complicated and requires a firm grasp of physics and chemistry, as well as mathematics and computer science. If you prepare yourself well, you may enjoy a long and fruitful career in meteorology. Even if you don't pursue meteorology, you now know a lot more about a subject that people talk about more than anything else—the weather!

Questions and Answers

After experimenting with weather phenomena, you should be able to select the correct answer to the questions listed below. (Answers appear at the bottom of the page.)

1. In the United States, the date on which a stick's shadow is shortest is closest to: (a) June 21; (b) December 21; (c) March 21; (d) September 21.

2. As we ascend into the atmosphere, the barometric pressure (a) decreases; (b) increases; (c) remains the same; (d) decreases then increases.

3. As we ascend into the atmosphere, the temperature usually: (a) decreases; (b) increases; (c) remains the same; (d) decreases then increases in the stratosphere.

4. Lightning may strike the same place (a) never; (b) often; (c) twice; (d) three times.

5. A cloud consists of (a) smoke; (b) water droplets or tiny ice crystals; (c) water vapor; (d) carbon dioxide.

6. Earth's seasons are caused by (a) the tilt of its axis; (b) its distance from the sun; (c) its distance from the moon; (d) its elliptical orbit.

7. Water in clouds may change from liquid to solid (a) only at 32°F (0°C); (b) at 32°F (0°C) and at temperatures well below 32°F (0°C); (c) at temperatures well above 32°F (0°C); (d) water in clouds never freezes.

8. Compared with humid air, dry air is (a) less dense; (b) more dense; (c) of equal density; (d) always warmer.

Answers: 1. a 2. a 3. d 4. b 5. b 6. a 7. b 8. b

Appendix

SCIENCE SUPPLY COMPANIES

Carolina Biological Supply Company
2700 York Road
Burlington, NC 27215-3398
(800) 334-5551
http://www.carolina.com

Connecticut Valley Biological
Supply Company
82 Valley Road
P.O. Box 326
Southampton, MA 01073
(800) 628-7748
http://www.ctvalleybio.com

Delta Education
80 Northwest Boulevard
P.O. Box 3000
Nashua, NH 03061-3000
(800) 442-5444
http://www.delta-education.com

Edmund Scientifics
60 Pearce Avenue
Tonawanda, NY 14150-6711
(800) 728-6999
http://scientificsonline.com

Educational Innovations, Inc.
362 Main Avenue
Norwalk, CT 06851
(888) 912-7474
http://www.teachersource.com

Fisher Science Education
4500 Turnberry Drive
Hanover Park, IL 60133
(800) 955-1177
http://www.fisheredu.com

Frey Scientific
100 Paragon Parkway
Mansfield, OH 44903
(800) 225-3739
http://www.freyscientific.com/

NASCO-Fort Atkinson
901 Janesville Avenue
P.O. Box 901
Fort Atkinson, WI 53538-0901
(800) 558-9595
http://www.nascofa.com/

NASCO-Modesto
4825 Stoddard Road
P.O. Box 3837
Modesto, CA 95352-3837
(800) 558-9595
http://www.nascofa.com

Sargent-Welch/VWR Scientific
P.O. Box 5229
Buffalo Grove, IL 60089-5229
(800) 727-4386
http://www.sargentwelch.com

Science Kit & Boreal Laboratories
777 East Park Drive
P.O. Box 5003
Tonawanda, NY 14150
(800) 828-7777
http://sciencekit.com

Ward's Natural Science
P.O. Box 92912
Rochester, NY 14692-9012
(800) 962-2660
http://www.wardsci.com

Further Reading

Adams, Richard, and Robert Gardner. *More Ideas for Science Projects*. Revised Edition. Danbury, Conn.: Franklin Watts, 1998.

Breen, Mark, and Kathleen Friestad. *The Kid's Book of Weather Forecasting: Build a Weather Station, Read the Sky, and Make Predictions*. Charlotte, Vt.: Williamson Publishing Co., 2000.

Cosgrove, Brian. *Weather*. New York: Dorling Kindersley, 2001.

Gardner, Robert. *Science Fair Projects—Planning, Presenting, Succeeding*. Springfield, N.J.: Enslow Publishers, Inc., 1998.

Scholastic Atlas of Weather. New York: Scholastic Reference, 2004.

Internet Addresses

The Franklin Institute Science Museum. *Franklin's Forecast*. © 1997. <http://www.fi.edu/weather>

University of Illinois at Urbana-Champaign. *The Weather World 2010 Project*. "Meteorology" <http://ww2010.atmos.uiuc.edu/(Gh)/guides/mtr/home.rxml>

The Weather Channel. *Weatherclassroom.com*. © 1995–2004. <http://www.weatherclassroom.com/home_students.php>

Index

A
absorption of solar energy
    effect of angle, 70–72
    effect of color, 81–82
air
    density and temperature, 63, 75–77
    movement affected by temperature, 73, 74–75
    percentage of oxygen in, 34–39
    and sky, 39–40
    stable and unstable, 92–94
    weight of, 25, 63
air currents, 91–92
air pressure, 25–27, 31
    measuring, 27–30
anemometer, 15, 16–17
aneroid barometer, 29–30, 31
atmospheric pressure, 25, 28

B
barometer
    aneroid, 29–30, 31
    the first, 27–28
barometric pressure, 28, 63
Beaufort scale, 17–19

C
clouds, 105–106
    and condensation nuclei, 107–108, 109–110
    and formation of rain and snow, 109
    ingredients needed to form, 106–108
    making, 108–110
    types of, 112–114
color absorption and radiant energy, 81–82, 83
colors in the sky, 40–42
Coriolis effect, 97–101, 116

D
density and temperature of air, 75–77, 94
dew point, 52–53
    finding by experiment, 54–57, 58
dispersion, 46

E
Earth's atmosphere, 32
    layers of, 32–34
    makeup of air, 34–40
    sunlight and colors, 40–42, 43–44
Earth's path around Sun, 66–68
Earth's source of heat, 65–66
evaporation of water, 52, 59, 84, 91
    affecting factors, 88–90
expansion of gas and temperature, 106, 107

F
forecasting weather, 122–123
formation of rain and snow, 109

G
Gulf Stream, 100

H
humidity, 52–53
    absolute, 55–56, 57
    and density of air, 63
    measuring with a hygrometer, 59–62
    relative, 54–56, 57, 60, 62
hurricanes, 115–118
hydrologic cycle, 83–84
    models of, 85–87
hygrometer, 59–62

I
infrared radiation, 76–77

J
jet streams, 103–104, 119

K
keeping daily weather records, 64–65

L
lightning, 115
    producing a mini-stroke, 118
    and thunder, 118–119
liquid tornadoes, 120–121

M
making thunder and lightning, 118–119
making weather instruments, 13–22

measuring rainfall, 20–21
meteorologists, 9–10, 23, 32, 92, 103, 112, 123

P
percentage of oxygen in air, 34–36, 37–39

R
radiant energy
    absorption by water and sand, 77–80
    effect of color on absorption, 81–82, 83
rainbows, 43–49
    different colors, 46, 48
    formation of natural, 46, 49
    from bending light with water, 45–46, 47
    from a hose, 43
    from a mirror in water, 44
raindrops, 109
rainfall content of snow, 22–23
refraction, 46
    of light by water in a cup, 50–51
    and making a rainbow, 45–49
    of sunrise and sunset, 50–51
relative humidity, 54

S
safety, 7–8
scattered light, 40–42
    and sky's color, 41–42
    and sun's color, 41–42
science fairs, 6–7
seasons, 66–73
sling psychrometer, 60
snow depth in terms of rainfall, 22–23
solar energy, 65–66
    Earth's absorption of, 76–83
    and the water cycle, 83–84
sun
    affect on Earth's air, 73
    and changing seasons, 66–68
    effect of angle on absorption of radiant energy, 70–72
    effect of angle on temperature, 68–70
    energy absorbed by Earth, 76–73
    refraction and appearance of, 50
sunlight
    and temperature of summer and winter, 68–70

T
temperature, 24
    of air, 24
    effect on density of air, 75–77
    effect on volume of air, 74–75
    and expansion of gas, 106
thermometer, 24
thunder, 115
    and lightning, 118–119
thunderstorms, 114–115
tornadoes, 119–120
    making with a liquid, 120–121
Torricelli, Evangelista, 27–29
transfer of energy to water and soil, 77–80
Tropic of Capricorn, 68–70

U
ultraviolet light, 33

V
vacuum, 25, 28
virtual vacuum, 50
volume of air and temperature, 74–75

W
water cycle, 83–84
    models of, 85–87
water vapor, 39–40, 52–54, 106, 107, 109
weather fronts, 10–12
weather instruments, 24–30
    aneroid barometer, 29–30, 31
    barometer, 27–30
    thermometer, 24
weather instruments you can make, 13–14
    anemometer, 15, 16–17
    rain gauge, 20–22
    wind vane, 14–16
weather maps, 10–12
weather station and records, 13–14, 64–65
white light, 41, 44, 46
winds, 94
    cause of, 94–96
    and Earth's rotation, 97–101, 102
    and friction, 96
    jet streams, 103–104
    measuring speed and direction, 14–16